D1033898

250 best
cookie
recipes

250 best cookie recipes

Esther Brody

Robert
ROSE

Dedication
To my daughter, Lisa Michelle
To my son, Leonard Jason
In memory of my parents,
Mary and Louis Goldstein

The 250 Best Cookie Recipes
Text copyright © 2001, 2013 Esther Brody
Photographs copyright © 2001, 2013 Robert Rose Inc. (except as noted below)
Cover and text design © 2001, 2013 Robert Rose Inc.

No part of this publication may be reproduced, stored in a retrieval system or transmitted, in any form or by any means, without the prior written consent of the publisher or a licence from the Canadian Copyright Licensing Agency (Access Copyright). For an Access Copyright licence, visit www.accesscopyright.ca or call toll-free: 1-800-893-5777.

For complete cataloguing information, see page 184

Disclaimer
The recipes in this book have been carefully tested by our kitchen and our tasters. To the best of our knowledge, they are safe and nutritious for ordinary use and users. For those people with food or other allergies, or who have special food requirements or health issues, please read the suggested contents of each recipe carefully and determine whether or not they may create a problem for you. All recipes are used at the risk of the consumer.

We cannot be responsible for any hazards, loss or damage that may occur as a result of any recipe use.

For those with special needs, allergies, requirements or health problems, in the event of any doubt, please contact your medical adviser prior to the use of any recipe.

Design and Production: Joseph Gisini and Martina Hwang/PageWave Graphics Inc.
Editors: Judith Finlayson and Carol Sherman
Copy Editor: Launie Lapp
Photography (except iStock as noted below):
  Cover Photography: Colin Erricson
  Cover Associate Photographer: Matt Johannsson
  Cover Food Stylist: Kathryn Robertson
  Interior Photography: Mark T. Shapiro
  Interior Food Stylist: Kate Bush
  Interior Food Art Direction: Sharon Matthews
  Prop Stylist: Charlene Erricson
Additional Interior photography: Dad's Favorite Chocolate Chip Cookies ©iStockphoto.com/SensorSpot; Golden Coconut Macaroons ©iStockphoto.com/robynmac; Mexican Wedding Cakes ©iStockphoto.com/viennetta; The Refrigerator Cookie ©iStockphoto.com/1MoreCreative; Cranberry Pistachio Biscotti ©iStockphoto.com/ma3; Homemade Ladyfingers ©iStockphoto.com/lucop; Ice-Cream Sandwiches ©iStockphoto.com/Kursad; Cream Cheese Shortbread ©iStockphoto.com/Yulia_Davidovich

Cover Image: The Original Tollhouse Cookie (page 24) and Traditional Peanut Butter Cookies (page 43)

We acknowledge the financial support of the Government of Canada through the Book Publishing Industry Development Program (BPIDP) for our publishing activities.

Published by Robert Rose Inc.
120 Eglinton Avenue East, Suite 800, Toronto, Ontario, Canada M4P 1E2
Tel: (416) 322-6552 Fax: (416) 322-6936
www.robertrose.ca

Printed and bound in Canada

1 2 3 4 5 6 7 8 9 MP 21 20 19 18 17 16 15 14 13

Contents

Introduction

WHO DOESN'T REMEMBER THE WONDERFUL, warm aroma coming from the kitchen as Mom was baking cookies? I wanted to gobble them up as soon as they came out of the oven but Mom always made us wait until they were cool enough to eat or she said we would get a stomachache.

I can remember coming home from school, walking into the house with my sisters and smelling the irresistible, magnificent aroma of cinnamon buns baking in the oven. Mom would take any leftover scraps of dough, roll them into a huge, flat cookie, sprinkle it with sugar and cinnamon and bake the cookie specially for us. It was my favorite cookie and still brings back many wonderful memories of my childhood.

Everyone loves cookies – young and old. Most cookies can be stored at room temperature for several days, or even weeks, if they don't disappear first. Everyone I know has a cookie jar sitting on the counter within easy reach. I find that using a cookie tin, with an airtight lid, helps cookies to keep that freshly baked flavor. Most cookies will freeze well, but they should be cooled completely before being placed in tins or containers. I always place a sheet of waxed paper between each layer.

Baking cookies can be a fun time. I remember years ago hearing about "Cookie Swaps" and later participated in a few of these myself. It has become a popular event, especially at Christmas time. Here's how it works. You bake one dozen cookies for each guest coming to the Swap. For example, if there will be 10 ladies participating, you would bake 10 dozen of say, your Peanut Butter Cookies. You'll come home with 10 dozen different cookies, one dozen of each kind brought by the other guests. It is a wise idea to bake your cookies a few days ahead so you won't be overwhelmed the day of the Swap. If you invite less than eight guests you really don't get enough variety in cookies, but if you have more than 12 guests, it would be too much baking for each person.

So, eight to 12 guests seems to work out best.

Decide in advance what type of cookie you will be bringing and let the hostess know so that there won't be a lot of duplication. I have one cookie recipe that everyone just assumes I should bring, my Chocolate Chip Komish Bread cookies (or miniscotti). In one Cookie Swap that I attended, a lady I had worked with brought some store-bought cookies and, needless to say, was never invited again. So, the cookies have to be homemade.

The wrapping is all part of the fun. Place each dozen cookies into 10 decorated bags, or some other unique wrapping, like baskets, decorative tins, plastic or freezer bags tied with colored ribbons. It's a great idea, especially for busy women, a perfect excuse to have a party, but also a way to get together with old and new friends to enjoy sharing your favorite cookies and recipes. So have lots of recipe cards and pens ready.

Another way to enjoy your special or favorite cookies is to make a cookie crust for pies, or any other desserts requiring a dough crust. You could use chocolate cookies, vanilla wafers, graham wafers or gingersnap cookies just to name a few. Crush the cookies into fine crumbs, about $1^1/_2$ cups (375 mL). Stir in melted butter or margarine, about $^1/_4$ cup (50 mL) and press into your pie plate. This type of crust can be chilled without baking, or baked at 350°F (180°C) for 10 minutes and then cooled.

Cookies are usually made from simple ingredients and are very versatile. They can be eaten at your leisure time, or when you are on the run it's great to be able to grab some cookies, take them with you in the car, in your briefcase, etc. to enjoy later. They're great also for coffee breaks, snacks or desserts, and most recipes are easy enough for even a novice cook to attempt as long as you follow the instructions. There is no limit in the way in which recipes can be varied according to your own taste. Happy Baking!
— ESTHER BRODY

Tips for Making Perfect Cookies

One of the beauties of making cookies is that you don't need special equipment. Cookie dough can be mixed by hand in a large bowl with a wooden spoon. It can also be prepared in an electric mixer or a food processor. As long as you've followed a tried-and-true recipe, all these methods produce equally delicious results.

The Right Equipment

Although most cookies are easy to prepare, following certain rules will guarantee outstanding results. For instance, I strongly recommend investing in heavy-duty cookie sheets. Likely they will cost a bit more than some, but I think they are worth it, because they won't rust and your cookies will bake more evenly. Cookie sheets differ from baking pans as they don't have sides, which allows the heat to circulate around the cookies, helping to ensure more even baking. If you don't have heavy-duty baking sheets, I recommend lowering the temperature of your oven by 25°F (10°C).

Getting Started

1. Another secret to successful baking is paying close attention to the recipe. Before you begin, read the recipe carefully and assemble all the necessary equipment and ingredients. Adjust oven racks to the desired level and 15 minutes before you want to bake, preheat the oven to the required temperature.

2. Don't make ingredient substitutions and don't double or halve the recipe unless it states that you can do so.

3. Shortening, butter, margarine and occasionally vegetable oil, all work equally well depending upon which the recipe specifies. I do not recommend the use of spreads sold in tubs for baking, as these products contain a higher percentage of water than solid fats. Cookies made from spreads will expand too much and will not brown as well as those made from more solid fats. They will also be tough and more likely to stick to the cookie sheet.

4. If a recipe calls for shortening, be aware that substituting butter or margarine will produce different results. Because butter and margarine melt more quickly than shortening, cookies made from butter will lose their shape and spread out more. Cookies made from shortening hold their shape better.

5. Remove shortening, butter or margarine from the refrigerator to soften 1 hour before mixing, unless the recipe specifies the use of cold butter.

6. Always use large size eggs when baking.

7. Since eggs separate more easily when they are cold, separate the yolks from the whites as soon as you take them out of the refrigerator. Return yolks to refrigerator until ready to use and if not using immediately, cover with cold water. (Drain off water before using the yolks in a recipe.) If beating whites, allow them to come to room temperature for 5 to 10 minutes before beating. Do not leave eggs at room temperature for longer than 1 hour.

8. Make sure your ingredients are fresh:
   - Purchase ground spices in small amounts and store tightly sealed in a cool, dry place. Replace ground spices annually.
   - Ensure that leavening agents such as baking soda and baking powder are still functional. Baking soda will keep for up to $1\frac{1}{2}$ years in a glass jar with a tight lid or in its original container. To test to make sure it is still active, mix 1 tbsp (15 mL) baking soda in $\frac{1}{2}$ cup (125 mL) cold water. Add 1 tsp (5 mL) vinegar. If the mixture doesn't fizz, discard the baking soda. To test if baking powder is still active, dissolve 1 tsp (5 mL) baking powder in $\frac{1}{3}$ cup (75 mL) hot tap water. The mixture should bubble up vigorously.
   - Buy seeds and nuts from a "bulk" purveyor with rapid turnover and store them in the refrigerator.
   - Keep marshmallows in the freezer.
   - Check the "best before" date on ingredients such as peanut butter, sour cream and yogurt.

9. Prepare cookie sheets or pans, if necessary. Place a dab of shortening on a piece of waxed paper and spread it over the cookie sheet. Grease cookie sheets only if the recipe specifies. Unnecessary greasing will cause some cookies to spread too much. As a general rule of thumb, dough containing a high proportion of shortening is baked on ungreased sheets. If the recipe indicates the sheet should be greased I recommend the use of shortening. In my opinion, butter, margarine or oil may cause cookies to stick. Instead of greasing sheets you can line the sheet with parchment or waxed paper cut to fit. Or, if a recipe calls for lightly greased, spraying with a vegetable spray is acceptable.

Mixing for Best Results

1. Measure ingredients carefully and accurately. Use measuring cups with a flat rim for dry ingredients so they can easily be leveled off. To measure less than $1/4$ cup (50 mL) use standard measuring spoons. Fill cups or spoons to overflowing, then level off using a straight-edged knife or spatula. Do not pack or bang on the table.

2. Unless a recipe calls for "sifted" flour, in which case it should be sifted first, then measured, flour is not sifted before it is measured. If a recipe calls for "sifting" the dry ingredients together, there is no need to sift the flour prior to measuring. Just sift all pre-measured ingredients together and proceed with the recipe.

3. If a recipe calls for "firmly packed" brown sugar, spoon it into a measuring cup, pack it down firmly with the back of a spoon, then level off.

4. Shortening, butter or margarine that is not sold in stick form should be measured in a cup that holds the exact amount when leveled off. Press firmly into the cup so that no air holes are left. Level off and scoop out.

5. Before mixing dough, combine dry ingredients such as flour, baking powder, baking soda and salt, in a bowl and mix thoroughly to ensure they are well blended.

6. If a recipe calls for extracts or flavorings, mix them in after the butter and sugar have been creamed, (after eggs have been beaten in, if using) so they will be well incorporated into the dough.

7. Roll dough out on a floured board unless otherwise specified.

8. When making cut cookies, dip the cookie cutter in flour so it won't stick to the dough. Cut the cookies as close together as possible, to reduce the quantity of leftover scraps to re-roll, as the more the dough is handled, the less tender your cookies will be.

9. Ensure that all cookies in a batch are the same size and shape to ensure even cooking.

Helpful Baking Tips

1. Pay close attention to oven temperature as cookies bake in a very short time and quickly become overcooked. If your oven is hotter than mine, you may need to lower the temperature by 25°F (10°C) or shorten the suggested baking times. You will get a feel for how your oven bakes after making a couple of batches of cookies.

2. Adjusting the temperature of the dough can also help you to get the shape of cookies you want. If you want your cookies to maintain their shape during baking, chill them on the sheet for 15 minutes before placing in the oven and increase the oven temperature a few degrees. If you want the cookies to flatten, place them in the oven when the dough is at room temperature and lower the oven temperature a few degrees.

3. When baking, place the cookie sheet on the middle rack of your oven. Ensure that the sheet is narrower than the oven rack and that it doesn't touch the sides of the oven so the heat can circulate properly. For best results, bake only one sheet of cookies at a time.

4. Begin checking to see if your cookies are done a few minutes before the times suggested in the recipe, as oven temperatures vary and every extra minute can make a big difference to the quality of cookies. Cookies are better if they are under rather than overcooked. They should be a bit soft in the center when they are removed from the oven. Drop cookies are done if they spring back into shape when you touch one lightly with your finger. Crisp cookies are done when lightly browned.

5. In order to prevent overbaking, remove cookies from the sheet within 3 minutes of taking them out of the oven, unless the recipe specifies otherwise. Using a lifter, transfer warm cookies to a wire rack to cool.

Ingredient Methods

Toasting Nuts

To toast nuts, spread out in a single layer on a baking sheet and bake, at 350°F (180°C) for about 5 to 10 minutes, stirring or shaking the pan, once or twice, until lightly browned.

After toasting hazelnuts, place them on a clean tea towel and rub together vigorously to remove the skin.

Sugar–Cinnamon Mix

In a cup, mix together ¹/₄ cup (50 mL) granulated sugar and 1 tsp (5 mL) ground cinnamon. Store in a jar.

Melting Chocolate

The trick in melting chocolate is to ensure it doesn't seize. Therefore, it is important that the chocolate does not come in contact with water, which will cause it to solidify into a grainy mass.

To ensure that chocolate melts quickly and evenly on the stovetop, break it into small pieces or use chocolate chips and stir constantly. Chocolate should always be melted over low heat or in a double boiler or a bowl set on top of a saucepan of hot (not boiling) water.

Chocolate also melts well in the microwave. Use chocolate chips, squares (each 1 oz/28 g) or small chunks. Place in a microwaveable bowl, cover tightly with plastic wrap and microwave on High approximately 1 minute per ounce. (Times will vary depending upon the power of your microwave and the quantity of chocolate used.) Stir well.

If your chocolate seizes up when melting, add 1 tsp (5 mL) shortening for every 2 squares (2 oz/56 g) of chocolate used and stir well until the mixture is smooth and creamy. Do not use butter as it contains water.

I also recommend that you grease your measuring cup or saucepan before melting chocolate for easy removal.

Store chocolate, well wrapped in an airtight container. A gray/white color, called a bloom, will appear on the surface of chocolate if it is stored in a warm area. This does not affect the quality or taste of the chocolate and the chocolate will return to its normal color when melted.

Freezing Cookies and Dough

Most cookie dough can be frozen for up to six months and most cookies freeze well. To freeze cookies, cool completely and place in airtight freezer bags with a sheet of waxed paper between layers.

Storing Cookies

Most cookies can be stored at room temperature for up to three weeks in an airtight container with a tight-fitting lid. Crisp cookies should be stored in a container with a loose-fitting lid, unless you live in a humid climate, in which case they should be covered tightly. If crisp cookies do soften, heating them in a 300°F (150°C) oven for 5 minutes will crisp them up.

Cookie Troubleshooting

Problem: Cookies stick to your cookie sheet.

Check the recipe to see if the sheet should be greased. If not, there may be ingredients in the cookies, such as raisins, that are causing them to stick. In that case, transfer the cookies to a wire rack as soon as they come out of the oven so they won't have a chance to stick to the sheet.

Problem: Cookies crumble or break when you remove them from the cookie sheet.

The sheet should be greased or the cookies may have been left on the hot sheet too long after they were removed from the oven.

Problem: Cookies are too dry.

Ingredients may not have been measured properly or the eggs may not have been large enough. Also, the cookies may have overbaked.

Problem: Cookies spread out too much.

You may have used too much butter, shortening or liquid or too little flour. Always measure ingredients correctly in a standard measuring cup.

Problem: Cookies run into each other instead of baking separately.

You may have made the cookies too large and/or placed them too close together on the cookie sheet. Cookies should be the size indicated in the recipe and be placed far enough apart (most recipes suggest 2 inches (5 cm) for medium-sized cookies) to allow for the appropriate amount of spreading. A dough that is too thin will also spread more than usual. Check to make sure you've measured the ingredients correctly.

Problem: Cookies bake unevenly.

Use heavy-duty cookie sheets. Make sure all the cookies are the same size and that the cookie sheet is placed in the center of the oven on the middle rack. It should not touch the sides of the oven. Since the heat in the rear of the oven is usually more intense than in the front, turn the sheet around halfway through the baking process.

Problem: Cookies are too well done.

Check to ensure that your oven temperature is not too hot. Begin checking for doneness a couple of minutes before the suggested baking time. Make cookies the size specified in the recipe and place them the recommended distance apart on the sheet.

Problem: Cookies are burned on bottom only.

The cookie sheet may be placed too low in the oven. It should be centered on the middle rack. Use a light, rather than a dark-colored sheet, as those with a dark surface absorb heat that may cause cookie bottoms to brown.

Drop Cookies

Drop cookies are the most popular type of cookie as they are so easy to make. Dropped from a spoon, onto a cookie sheet, they spread out as they bake. Many of the most common cookies, such as traditional chocolate chip, oatmeal, meringues and macaroons, are drop cookies. But the ingredients for drop cookies can be varied to produce a wide range of delectable treats, from fruit-filled and frosted cookies to chunky hermits.

Oatmeal Cookies

Chocolate Chip Cookies

Chocolate Cookies

Coconut Cookies

Fruit Cookies

Frosted Cookies

Meringues

Filled Cookies

Other Drop Cookies

Oat Bran Raisin Cookies

This recipe makes a smaller batch of cookies than usual but it can be doubled, if desired.

²/₃ cup	uncooked oat bran cereal	160 mL
¹/₄ cup	old-fashioned rolled oats	50 mL
3 tbsp	all-purpose flour	45 mL
¹/₂ tsp	baking powder	2 mL
3 tbsp	softened margarine	45 mL
¹/₄ cup	firmly packed brown sugar	50 mL
1	egg white, lightly beaten	1
2 tsp	water	10 mL
¹/₄ tsp	vanilla	1 mL
2 tbsp	raisins	25 mL

Preheat oven to 350°F (180°C)
Greased cookie sheet

1. In a bowl, mix together oat bran, rolled oats, flour and baking powder.

2. In another bowl, beat together margarine and brown sugar until smooth and creamy. Stir in egg white, water and vanilla, mixing until thoroughly incorporated. Add flour mixture and mix well. Fold in raisins.

3. Drop by level tablespoonfuls (15 mL), about 2 inches (5 cm) apart, onto prepared cookie sheet. Using a fork or the bottom of a glass flatten slightly. Bake in preheated oven for 12 to 15 minutes or until bottoms are slightly browned. Cool on sheet for 3 minutes, then transfer to wire racks to cool completely.

Makes about one dozen

Wholesome Banana Granola Drops

1¹/₂ cups	all-purpose flour	375 mL
¹/₂ tsp	baking soda	2 mL
¹/₂ tsp	salt	2 mL
1 tsp	cinnamon	5 mL
¹/₂ cup	softened butter or margarine	125 mL
1 cup	firmly packed brown sugar	250 mL
1	egg	1
¹/₂ tsp	vanilla	2 mL
1 cup	mashed bananas	250 mL
1 cup	granola	250 mL

HINT: To keep bananas from turning brown, wrap individual bananas tightly in aluminum foil and refrigerate in the crisper drawer. This will slow down the ripening process.

Preheat oven to 375°F (190°C)
Greased cookie sheet

1. In a bowl, mix together flour, baking soda, salt and cinnamon.

2. In another bowl, beat butter and brown sugar until smooth and creamy. Add egg, vanilla and bananas and beat until well blended. Add flour mixture and mix well. Stir in granola.

3. Drop by tablespoonfuls (15 mL), about 2 inches (5 cm) apart, onto prepared cookie sheet. Bake in preheated oven for 12 minutes or until golden brown. Immediately transfer to wire racks to cool.

Makes about 4 dozen

Banana Oatmeal Drops

1½ cups	all-purpose flour	375 mL
1¾ cups	quick-cooking oats	425 mL
1 tsp	salt	5 mL
1 tsp	cinnamon	5 mL
½ tsp	baking soda	2 mL
¼ tsp	nutmeg	1 mL
¾ cup	softened shortening	175 mL
1 cup	firmly packed brown sugar	250 mL
1	egg	1
1 cup	mashed bananas	250 mL
½ cup	chopped pecans or walnuts	125 mL

Note: For a special treat, frost these cookies with Quick Banana Frosting or Creamy Lemon Frosting (see Recipes, below).

Preheat oven to 350°F (180°C)
Greased cookie sheet

1. In a bowl, mix together flour, oats, salt, cinnamon, baking soda and nutmeg.

2. In another bowl, beat shortening and brown sugar until smooth and creamy. Add egg and mashed bananas and mix well. Add flour mixture and mix well. Fold in nuts.

3. Drop by heaping teaspoonfuls (5 mL), about 2 inches (5 cm) apart, onto prepared cookie sheet. Bake in preheated oven for 12 to 15 minutes or until golden brown. Cool slightly on sheet, then transfer to wire racks to cool completely.

Makes about 5 dozen

Quick Banana Frosting

1	ripe mashed banana	1
½ tsp	almond extract	2 mL
2 cups	confectioner's (icing) sugar, sifted	500 mL

1. In a bowl, beat banana, almond extract and confectioner's sugar until blended and spreadable.

Creamy Lemon Frosting

¼ cup	softened butter or margarine	50 mL
¼ cup	softened shortening	50 mL
¼ tsp	salt	1 mL
1	egg	1
3 cups	confectioner's (icing) sugar, sifted	750 mL
¼ cup	light corn syrup	50 mL
3 tbsp	lemon juice	45 mL

1. In a bowl, beat butter and shortening until creamy. Beat in salt and egg. Gradually beat in confectioner's sugar. Then slowly add corn syrup and lemon juice, beating until fluffy and spreadable.

Apple Oatmeal Cookies

1³/₄ cups	all-purpose flour	425 mL
¹/₂ tsp	baking powder	2 mL
¹/₂ tsp	baking soda	2 mL
¹/₂ tsp	salt	2 mL
¹/₂ cup	quick-cooking oats	125 mL
¹/₂ tsp	nutmeg	2 mL
¹/₂ tsp	cinnamon	2 mL
¹/₂ cup	softened shortening	125 mL
1 cup	packed brown sugar	250 mL
2	eggs	2
1 cup	finely chopped peeled apples	250 mL
1 cup	raisins	250 mL
1 cup	chopped nuts	250 mL

HINT: To test if eggs are fresh, place them in a bowl of cold, salted water. They are fresh if they sink to the bottom and stay there.

Preheat oven to 400°F (200°C)
Greased cookie sheet

1. In a bowl, mix together flour, baking powder, baking soda, salt, oats, nutmeg and cinnamon.

2. In another bowl, beat shortening and brown sugar until smooth and creamy. Add eggs, one at a time, mixing until well incorporated. Mix in apples and raisins. Add flour mixture and mix well. Fold in nuts.

3. Drop by rounded teaspoonfuls (5 mL), about 2 inches (5 cm) apart, onto prepared cookie sheet. Bake in preheated oven for 10 to 12 minutes or until golden brown. Immediately transfer to wire racks to cool.

Makes about 6 dozen

Oatmeal Pudding Drops

1 cup	all-purpose flour	250 mL
1¹/₂ tsp	baking powder	7 mL
¹/₂ tsp	salt	2 mL
1	package (3 oz/85 g) Jello pudding, any flavor	1
³/₄ cup	softened shortening	175 mL
2 tbsp	granulated sugar	25 mL
1	egg	1
1 tsp	vanilla	5 mL
1 cup	old-fashioned rolled oats	250 mL

Preheat oven to 350°F (180°C)
Ungreased cookie sheet

1. In a bowl, sift together flour, baking powder and salt.

2. In another bowl, beat pudding powder, shortening, sugar, egg and vanilla until smooth and blended. Add flour mixture and mix well.

3. Drop by teaspoonfuls (5 mL), about 2 inches (5 cm) apart, onto cookie sheet. Bake in preheated oven for 15 minutes or until golden brown. Immediately transfer to wire racks to cool.

Makes about 3 dozen

Cranberry Orange Oatmeal Cookies

2 cups	all-purpose flour	500 mL
1 tsp	baking powder	5 mL
1/4 tsp	baking soda	1 mL
1/2 tsp	salt	2 mL
2 cups	quick-cooking oats	500 mL
1 cup	softened butter or margarine	250 mL
1 1/2 cups	granulated sugar	375 mL
2	eggs	2
1 tsp	vanilla	5 mL
1 cup	raisins	250 mL
1 cup	coarsely chopped cranberries, fresh or frozen	250 mL
1 tbsp	grated orange zest	15 mL

HINT: Freeze cranberries before chopping or grinding them to ease clean up.

Preheat oven to 375°F (190°C)
Greased cookie sheet

1. In a bowl, mix together flour, baking powder, baking soda, salt and oats.

2. In another bowl, beat butter or margarine and sugar until smooth and creamy. Beat in eggs, one at a time, until well incorporated. Mix in vanilla. Add flour mixture and mix well. Fold in raisins, cranberries and orange zest.

3. Drop by rounded teaspoonfuls (5 mL), about 2 inches (5 cm) apart, onto prepared cookie sheet. Bake in preheated oven for 10 to 12 minutes or until edges are lightly browned. Immediately transfer to wire racks to cool.

Makes about 5 dozen

Peanut Butter 'n' Honey Oatmeal Drops

1 1/2 cups	all-purpose flour	375 mL
1 tsp	baking soda	5 mL
1 tsp	salt	5 mL
1 1/2 cups	quick-cooking rolled oats	375 mL
1 1/2 cups	chunky peanut butter	375 mL
2 cups	liquid honey	500 mL
3	eggs	3
1 tbsp	water	15 mL
2 tsp	vanilla	10 mL
2 cups	raisins	500 mL

HINT: When you need to measure honey or syrup, grease the cup with cooking oil. If your recipe calls for oil, shortening or butter measure that ingredient first, then use the cup to measure out honey or syrup.

Preheat oven to 350°F (180°C)
Greased cookie sheet

1. In a bowl, mix together flour, baking soda, salt and oats.

2. In another bowl, mix together peanut butter, honey, eggs, water and vanilla until well blended. Add flour mixture and mix well. Fold in raisins. Refrigerate dough for 30 minutes until firm.

3. Drop by rounded teaspoonfuls (5 mL), about 2 inches (5 cm) apart, onto prepared cookie sheet. Bake in preheated oven for 12 to 15 minutes or until tops spring back when lightly touched. Immediately transfer to wire racks to cool.

Makes about 8 dozen

Homemade Oatmeal Macaroons

2	egg whites	2
3/4 cup	granulated sugar, divided	175 mL
1/2 cup	butter or margarine, melted	125 mL
2 cups	quick-cooking oats	500 mL
1/4 cup	all-purpose flour	50 mL

HINT: Overbaked cookies can be crumbled and sprinkled over ice cream or fresh fruit or used as a topping for fruit crumbles.

Preheat oven to 350°F (180°C)
Lightly greased cookie sheet

1. In a bowl, beat egg whites until soft peaks form. Gradually add 1/4 cup (50 mL) sugar, beating until stiff peaks form.

2. In another bowl, mix together remaining sugar, butter or margarine, oats and flour. Fold into beaten egg whites until well blended.

3. Drop by level tablespoonfuls (15 mL), about 1 inch (2.5 cm) apart, onto prepared cookie sheet. Bake in preheated oven for 10 to 12 minutes or until lightly browned. Immediately transfer to wire racks to cool.

Makes about 3 dozen

Peaches 'n' Cream Oatmeal Cookies

Although these cookies will taste better if made from freshly picked peaches, canned peaches make an acceptable substitute out of season.

1 1/2 cups	whole wheat flour	375 mL
2 1/2 cups	old-fashioned rolled oats	625 mL
2 tsp	baking powder	10 mL
1 tsp	salt	5 mL
2/3 cup	softened butter or margarine	160 mL
3/4 cup	granulated sugar	175 mL
3/4 cup	packed brown sugar	175 mL
2	eggs	2
1 1/2 tsp	vanilla	7 mL
3	diced peaches	3
3/4 cup	raisins (optional)	175 mL

HINT: To ripen fruits such as peaches, nectarines or plums, place the unripe fruit in a brown paper bag, close the bag and keep it on your kitchen counter or in an area away from direct sunlight or cold. It will be ripe in 1 to 3 days.

Preheat oven to 350°F (180°C)
Lightly greased cookie sheet

1. In a bowl, mix together flour, oats, baking powder and salt.

2. In another bowl, beat butter or margarine and sugars until smooth and creamy. Beat in eggs, one at a time, until incorporated. Stir in vanilla. Add flour mixture and mix well. Fold in peaches and raisins. Refrigerate dough for 30 minutes until firm.

3. Drop by rounded teaspoonfuls (5 mL), about 2 inches (5 cm) apart, onto prepared cookie sheet. Bake in preheated oven for 10 to 15 minutes or until golden brown. Immediately transfer to wire racks to cool.

Makes about 3 dozen

Chock-Full Oatmeal Cookies

2 cups	all-purpose flour	500 mL
1 tsp	baking soda	5 mL
1/2 tsp	salt	2 mL
1 cup	quick-cooking oats	250 mL
1/2 cup	softened butter	125 mL
1/2 cup	granulated sugar	125 mL
3/4 cup	packed brown sugar	175 mL
1	egg	1
2	egg whites	2
2 tsp	vanilla	10 mL
1 cup	semi-sweet chocolate chunks	250 mL
1/2 cup	dark raisins	125 mL

HINT: Always use large size eggs when baking cookies.

Preheat oven to 375°F (190°C)
Lightly greased cookie sheet

1. In a bowl, mix together flour, baking soda, salt and oats.

2. In another bowl, beat butter and sugars until smooth and creamy. Beat in egg, then egg whites, until incorporated. Stir in vanilla. Add flour mixture and mix well. Fold in chocolate and raisins until well combined.

3. Drop by level tablespoonfuls (15 mL), about 2 inches (5 cm) apart, onto prepared cookie sheet. Bake in preheated oven for 10 to 12 minutes or until golden brown. Immediately transfer to wire racks to cool.

Makes about 4 dozen

Golden Raisin Oat Cookies

2 cups	old-fashioned rolled oats	500 mL
1 cup	golden raisins	250 mL
2 cups	all-purpose flour	500 mL
1 tsp	baking soda	5 mL
1/2 tsp	salt	2 mL
1 cup	softened butter or margarine	250 mL
1 cup	packed, light brown sugar	250 mL
1 cup	granulated sugar	250 mL
2	eggs	2
2 tsp	vanilla	10 mL

HINT: To soften brown sugar that has hardened, add a slice of fresh bread. Close container tightly. The sugar will be soft in a few hours.

Preheat oven to 350°F (180°C)
Food processor
Ungreased cookie sheet

1. Using a food processor, pulse oats and raisins until coarsely ground. Add flour, baking soda and salt and pulse once or twice to combine.

2. In a bowl, beat butter or margarine and sugars until light and creamy. Beat in eggs, one at a time, until incorporated. Stir in vanilla. Add flour mixture and mix well.

3. Drop by tablespoonfuls (15 mL), about 2 inches (5 cm) apart, onto cookie sheet. Bake in preheated oven for 12 to 15 minutes or until golden brown. Immediately transfer to wire racks to cool.

Makes about 3 dozen

Peanut Butter Oat Cookies

1 cup	all-purpose flour	250 mL
1/2 tsp	baking powder	2 mL
1/2 tsp	baking soda	2 mL
1 1/2 cups	quick-cooking oats	375 mL
1/2 tsp	salt	2 mL
1/2 cup	softened butter	125 mL
1/2 cup	granulated sugar	125 mL
1 cup	lightly packed brown sugar	250 mL
1	egg	1
6 tbsp	crunchy peanut butter	90 mL
2 tbsp	water	25 mL
1/2 tsp	vanilla	2 mL

Preheat oven to 350°F (180°C)
Greased cookie sheet

1. In a bowl, mix together flour, baking powder, baking soda, oats and salt.

2. In another bowl, beat butter and sugars until smooth and creamy. Beat in egg, until incorporated. Add peanut butter, water and vanilla and mix until smooth. Add flour mixture and mix well.

3. Drop by rounded tablespoonfuls (15 mL), 2 inches (5 cm) apart, onto prepared cookie sheet. Using your hand or the back of a spoon, press down slightly to flatten. Bake in preheated oven for 15 minutes or until golden brown. Immediately transfer to wire racks to cool.

Makes about 4 dozen

Maple Walnut Oatmeal Cookies

1 cup	all-purpose flour	250 mL
3 cups	quick-cooking oats	750 mL
1/2 tsp	baking soda	2 mL
1/2 tsp	salt	2 mL
1/4 tsp	cinnamon	1 mL
3/4 cup	softened butter or butter-flavored shortening	175 mL
1 1/4 cups	firmly packed brown sugar	300 mL
1	egg	1
1 1/2 tsp	vanilla	7 mL
1 1/2 tsp	maple extract	7 mL
1/3 cup	milk	75 mL
1 cup	coarsely chopped walnuts	250 mL

Preheat oven to 375°F (190°C)
Greased cookie sheet

1. In a bowl, mix together flour, oats, baking soda, salt and cinnamon.

2. In another bowl, beat butter or shortening and brown sugar until smooth and creamy. Beat in egg until incorporated. Stir in vanilla, maple extract and milk and mix well. Add flour mixture and mix well. Fold in nuts.

3. Drop by rounded tablespoonfuls (15 mL), about 2 inches (5 cm) apart, onto prepared cookie sheet. Using your hand or the back of a spoon, press down slightly to flatten. Bake in preheated oven for 10 to 12 minutes or until lightly browned. Cool on sheet for 2 minutes, then transfer to wire racks to cool completely.

Makes about 2 1/2 dozen

HINT: If you ever have a recipe that calls for half an egg, beat one egg lightly and use 2 tbsp (25 mL).

Oatmeal Lace Pennies

1 cup	old-fashioned rolled oats	250 mL
1 cup	granulated sugar	250 mL
3 tbsp	all-purpose flour	45 mL
1/4 tsp	baking powder	1 mL
1/2 tsp	salt	2 mL
1	egg, beaten	1
1/2 cup	butter, melted	125 mL
1/2 tsp	vanilla	2 mL

Preheat oven to 350°F (180°C)
Cookie sheet lined with foil, bright side up

1. In a bowl, mix together oats, sugar, flour, baking powder and salt.

2. In another bowl, beat egg, butter and vanilla. Add flour mixture and mix well. (If dough seems too soft, chill for 15 to 20 minutes to firm.)

3. Drop by rounded teaspoonfuls (5 mL), about 2 inches (5 cm) apart, onto prepared cookie sheet. Bake in preheated oven for 8 to 10 minutes. Cool for 2 minutes on foil, then transfer to wire racks to cool completely.

Makes about 5 1/2 dozen

Easy Oatmeal Drop Cookies

1 cup	all-purpose flour	250 mL
1 tsp	baking powder	5 mL
1/2 tsp	salt	2 mL
3/4 cup	softened shortening	175 mL
1 cup	lightly packed brown sugar	250 mL
2	eggs, beaten	2
1 tsp	vanilla	5 mL
1/3 cup	milk, divided	75 mL
3 cups	old-fashioned rolled oats	750 mL

Preheat oven to 375°F (190°C)
Greased cookie sheet

1. In a bowl, mix together flour, baking powder and salt.

2. Using two knives, a pastry blender or the tips of your fingers, cut in shortening until mixture resembles coarse crumbs. Stir in sugar, eggs, vanilla and half the milk. Beat until the mixture is smooth and blended. Mix together remaining milk and oats and fold into mixture.

3. Drop by rounded teaspoonfuls (5 mL), about 2 inches (5 cm) apart, onto prepared cookie sheet. Bake in preheated oven for 12 to 15 minutes or until golden brown. Immediately transfer to wire racks to cool.

Makes about 4 dozen

VARIATIONS

Date–Nut Oatmeal Cookies
Add 1 cup (250 mL) chopped dates and 1 cup (250 mL) chopped nuts to the batter along with the oats.

Chocolate Chip Oatmeal Cookies
Add 1 cup (250 mL) chocolate chips to the batter along with the oats.

Raisin Oatmeal Cookies
Add 3/4 cup (175 mL) raisins to the batter along with the oats.

Old-Fashioned Raisin Nut Oatmeal Cookies

1 cup	water	250 mL
1 cup	raisins	250 mL
2¹/₂ cups	all-purpose flour	625 mL
1 tsp	baking soda	5 mL
¹/₂ tsp	baking powder	2 mL
1 tsp	salt	5 mL
1 tsp	cinnamon	5 mL
¹/₂ tsp	cloves	2 mL
2 cups	quick-cooking rolled oats	500 mL
¹/₂ cup	chopped nuts	125 mL
³/₄ cup	softened shortening or butter	175 mL
1¹/₂ cups	granulated sugar	325 mL
2	eggs	2
1 tsp	vanilla	5 mL

Preheat oven to 400°F (200°C)
Ungreased cookie sheet

1. In a saucepan, over medium heat, bring water and raisins to a boil. Simmer for 15 to 20 minutes or until raisins are plump. Drain, reserving liquid. If necessary, add water so liquid measures ¹/₂ cup (125 mL). Set raisins aside.

2. In a bowl, mix together flour, baking soda, baking powder, salt, cinnamon, cloves, oats, nuts and reserved raisins.

3. In another bowl, beat shortening or butter and sugar until smooth and creamy. Beat in eggs, one at a time. Stir in vanilla and reserved raisin liquid. Add flour mixture and mix well.

4. Drop by rounded teaspoonfuls (5 mL), 2 inches (5 cm) apart, onto cookie sheet. Bake in preheated oven for 8 to 10 minutes or until lightly browned. Cool for 3 minutes on sheet, then transfer to wire racks to cool completely.

Makes about 6 dozen

The Original Tollhouse Cookie

1 cup	all-purpose flour	250 mL
¹/₂ tsp	baking soda	2 mL
¹/₂ tsp	salt	2 mL
²/₃ cup	softened butter	160 mL
1 cup	lightly packed brown sugar	250 mL
1	egg, beaten	1
1¹/₂ tsp	vanilla	7 mL
¹/₂ cup	old-fashioned rolled oats	125 mL
¹/₂ cup	chopped nuts	125 mL
1 cup	chocolate chips or chunks	250 mL

Preheat oven to 375°F (190°C)
Greased cookie sheet

1. In a bowl, mix together flour, baking soda and salt.

2. In another bowl, beat butter and brown sugar until smooth and creamy. Beat in egg until well incorporated. Stir in vanilla. Add flour mixture and mix well. Stir in rolled oats, nuts and chocolate chips or chunks.

3. Drop by rounded teaspoonfuls (5 mL), about 2 inches (5 cm) apart, onto prepared cookie sheet. Bake in preheated oven for 10 minutes or until golden brown. Immediately transfer to wire racks to cool.

Makes about 5 dozen

Chocolate Mint Chip Drops

2 cups	all-purpose flour	500 mL
3/4 cup	unsweetened cocoa	175 mL
1 tsp	baking soda	5 mL
1/4 tsp	salt	1 mL
1 cup	softened butter	250 mL
3/4 cup	granulated sugar	175 mL
1 cup	packed light brown sugar	250 mL
2	eggs	2
2 tsp	vanilla	10 mL
2 cups	mint chocolate chips	500 mL

NOTE: You can also substitute chocolate chips for the mint chocolate chips and add 1/4 tsp (1 mL) mint extract along with the vanilla.

Preheat oven to 375°F (190°C)
Ungreased cookie sheet

1. In a bowl, combine flour, cocoa, baking soda and salt.

2. In another bowl, beat butter and sugars until smooth and creamy. Add eggs, one at a time, mixing until well incorporated. Stir in vanilla. Add flour mixture and mix well. Fold in mint chocolate chips.

3. Drop by heaping teaspoonfuls (5 mL), about 2 inches (5 cm) apart, onto cookie sheet. Bake in preheated oven for 9 to 12 minutes or until cookies are crisp. Cool on sheet for 2 minutes, then transfer to wire racks to cool completely.

Makes about 5 dozen

Cream Cheese Chocolate Chip Cookies

1	package (10 oz/ 300 g) mini chocolate chips, divided	1
2 1/4 cups	all-purpose flour	550 mL
1 1/2 tsp	baking soda	7 mL
1/2 cup	softened butter	125 mL
1	package (8 oz/250 g) softened cream cheese	1
1 1/2 cups	granulated sugar	375 mL
1	egg	1
1/2 cup	chopped nuts	125 mL

NOTE: Try making these cookies using raspberry or other flavored chips. For an added treat, drizzle melted chocolate chips over top of the cookies as soon as they come out of the oven.

Preheat oven to 350°F (180°C)
Ungreased cookie sheet

1. In a saucepan over very low heat, melt 1 cup (250 mL) chocolate chips.

2. In a bowl, mix together flour and baking soda.

3. In another bowl, beat butter, cream cheese and sugar until smooth and creamy. Beat in egg until well incorporated. Beat in melted chocolate until well combined. Add flour mixture and mix well. Fold in nuts and remaining chocolate chips.

4. Drop by tablespoonfuls (15 mL), about 2 inches (5 cm) apart, onto cookie sheet. Bake in preheated oven for 10 to 12 minutes or until cookies are firm around the edges. Immediately transfer to wire racks to cool.

Makes about 4 dozen

Dad's Favorite Chocolate Chip Cookies

3¹/₂ cups	all-purpose flour	875 mL
1 tsp	salt	5 mL
1 tsp	baking soda	5 mL
²/₃ cup	softened shortening	160 mL
²/₃ cup	softened butter or margarine	160 mL
1 cup	packed brown sugar	250 mL
1 cup	granulated sugar	250 mL
2	eggs	2
2 tsp	vanilla	10 mL
2	packages (12 oz/375 g) semi-sweet chocolate chips	2
1 cup	chopped nuts (optional)	250 mL

Preheat oven to 375°F (190°C)
Ungreased cookie sheet

1. In a bowl, mix together flour, salt and baking soda.

2. In another bowl, beat shortening, butter or margarine and sugars until smooth and creamy. Beat in eggs, one at a time, until incorporated. Stir in vanilla. Add flour mixture and mix well. Fold in chocolate chips and nuts, if using.

3. Drop by rounded teaspoonfuls (5 mL), about 2 inches (5 cm) apart, onto cookie sheet. Bake in preheated oven for 10 minutes or until lightly browned. Cool on sheet for 2 minutes, then transfer to wire racks to cool completely.

Makes about 7 dozen

Chocolate Chip Raspberry Cream Cheese Drops

2¹/₂ cups	all-purpose flour	625 mL
1 tsp	baking soda	5 mL
¹/₂ cup	softened butter or margarine	125 mL
1¹/₂ cups	granulated sugar	375 mL
1	package (8 oz/ 250 g) softened cream cheese	1
1	egg	1
1 cup	semi-sweet chocolate chips, melted (see page 11)	250 mL
1 cup	mini raspberry chips	250 mL

Preheat oven to 350°F (180°C)
Ungreased cookie sheet

1. In a bowl, mix together flour and baking soda.

2. In another bowl, beat butter or margarine, sugar and cream cheese until smooth. Beat in egg and melted chocolate until well blended. Add flour mixture and mix well. Fold in raspberry chips.

3. Drop by rounded teaspoonfuls (5 mL), about 2 inches (5 cm) apart, onto cookie sheet. Bake in preheated oven for 12 to 15 minutes or until tops of cookies spring back when lightly touched. Immediately transfer to wire racks to cool.

Makes about 2 dozen

Orange Chocolate Chip Cookies

1 cup	all-purpose flour	250 mL
1/4 tsp	salt	1 mL
1/2 cup	softened butter or margarine	125 mL
1/2 cup	granulated sugar	125 mL
1	package (4 oz/125 g) softened cream cheese	1
1	egg	1
1 tsp	vanilla	5 mL
1 tsp	orange zest	5 mL
1 cup	semi-sweet chocolate chips	250 mL

Preheat oven to 350°F (180°C)
Ungreased cookie sheet

1. In a bowl, mix together flour and salt.

2. In another bowl, beat butter or margarine, sugar and cream cheese until smooth. Beat in egg until incorporated. Stir in vanilla and orange zest. Add flour mixture and mix well. Fold in chocolate chips.

3. Drop by teaspoonfuls (5 mL), about 1 inch (2.5 cm) apart, onto cookie sheet. Bake in preheated oven for 15 minutes or until edges are lightly browned. Immediately transfer to wire racks to cool.

Makes about 3 dozen

German Chocolate Cake Cookies

1/2 cup	softened butter or margarine	125 mL
2	eggs	2
1	package (18 1/4 oz/515 g) chocolate cake mix	1
2 tbsp	all-purpose flour	25 mL
18	glazed maraschino cherries, halved	18

NOTE: For a treat, ice the cookies while they are still warm with Chocolate Icing (see Recipe, page 44).

HINT: For a quick, delicious frosting, add maple syrup to confectioner's sugar and stir until thick and creamy. It's especially good on chocolate or mocha cookies.

Preheat oven to 350°F (180°C)
Greased cookie sheet

1. In a bowl, cream butter until smooth. Beat in eggs, one at a time, until incorporated. Mix in cake mix and flour. (Dough should be stiff.)

2. Drop by rounded teaspoonfuls (5 mL), about 2 inches (5 cm) apart, onto prepared cookie sheet. Press a cherry half into the top of each cookie. Bake in preheated oven for 10 to 12 minutes. Immediately transfer to wire racks to cool.

Makes 3 dozen

Chocolate Buttermilk Pyramids

2 cups	all-purpose flour	500 mL
$1/2$ cup	cocoa	125 mL
2 tsp	baking powder	10 mL
$1/2$ tsp	baking soda	2 mL
1 tsp	salt	5 mL
$1/2$ cup	softened shortening	125 mL
1 cup	granulated sugar	250 mL
2	eggs	2
$1/2$ tsp	vanilla	2 mL
1 cup	buttermilk	250 mL
	Confectioner's (icing) sugar, sifted (optional)	

HINT: Keep a sugar shaker filled with confectioner's sugar available for dusting cookies.

Preheat oven to 350°F (180°C)
Ungreased cookie sheet

1. In a bowl, mix together flour, cocoa, baking powder, baking soda and salt.

2. In another bowl, beat shortening and sugar until smooth and creamy. Beat in eggs, one at a time, until well incorporated. Stir in vanilla. Add flour mixture alternately with buttermilk, mixing well after each addition.

3. Drop by rounded teaspoonfuls (5 mL), about 2 inches (5 cm) apart, onto cookie sheet. Bake in preheated oven for 12 to 15 minutes or until edges are lightly browned. Immediately transfer to wire racks to cool. Dust warm cookies with confectioner's sugar, if desired.

Makes about 4 dozen

Golden Coconut Macaroons

2	egg whites	2
$1/2$ tsp	vanilla	2 mL
2 tbsp	cake flour	25 mL
$1/2$ cup	granulated sugar	125 mL
$1/4$ tsp	salt	1 mL
2 cups	shredded coconut	500 mL

VARIATIONS

Cherry Coconut Macaroons
Add $1/2$ cup (125 mL) chopped candied cherries along with the coconut.

Chocolate Chip Macaroons
Substitute $1/2$ cup (125 mL) chocolate chips for the coconut.

Cornflake Macaroons
Substitute 2 cups (500 mL) cornflakes for the coconut.

Hazelnut Macaroons
Substitute 2 cups (500 mL) finely ground hazelnuts for the coconut.

Preheat oven to 350°F (180°C)
Cookie sheet lined with waxed or parchment paper or foil

1. In a bowl, beat egg whites and vanilla until soft peaks form.

2. In another bowl, sift together flour, sugar and salt. Fold in beaten egg whites, then fold in coconut, blending thoroughly.

3. Drop by rounded teaspoonfuls (5 mL), about 2 inches (5 cm) apart, onto prepared cookie sheet. Bake in preheated oven for 20 minutes or until golden brown. Immediately transfer to wire racks to cool.

Makes about $1 1/2$ dozen

Ambrosia Coconut Drops

2 cups	all-purpose flour	500 mL
1 tsp	baking soda	5 mL
$1/2$ tsp	salt	2 mL
$1/2$ cup	softened butter	125 mL
$1^{1}/_{4}$ cups	granulated sugar	300 mL
2	eggs	2
1 cup	shredded coconut	250 mL
1 tbsp	orange zest	15 mL
$1/2$ cup	orange juice	125 mL

Preheat oven to 350°F (180°C)
Lightly greased cookie sheet

1. In a bowl, sift together flour, baking soda and salt.

2. In another bowl, beat butter and sugar until smooth and creamy. Beat in eggs, one at a time, until incorporated. Add flour mixture and mix well.

3. In a small bowl, combine coconut and orange zest and juice. Fold into batter.

4. Drop by teaspoonfuls (5 mL), about 2 inches (5 cm) apart, onto prepared cookie sheet. Bake in preheated oven for 10 to 12 minutes or until golden brown. Transfer to wire racks.

Makes about 4 dozen

Carrot Coconut Drops

2 cups	all-purpose flour	500 mL
2 tsp	baking powder	10 mL
$1/2$ tsp	salt	2 mL
$1/2$ cup	softened shortening	125 mL
$1/2$ cup	softened butter	125 mL
$3/4$ cup	granulated sugar	175 mL
2	eggs	2
1 cup	mashed cooked carrots	250 mL
$3/4$ cup	shredded coconut	175 mL

NOTE: If desired, these cookies may be frosted with Orange–Butter Icing (see Recipe, below).

Preheat oven to 400°F (200°C)
Lightly greased cookie sheet

1. In a bowl, mix together flour, baking powder and salt.

2. In another bowl, beat shortening, butter and sugar until smooth and creamy. Beat in eggs, one at a time, until incorporated. Stir in carrots. Add flour mixture and mix well. Fold in coconut.

3. Drop by teaspoonfuls (5 mL), about 2 inches (5 cm) apart, onto prepared cookie sheet. Bake in preheated oven for 8 to 10 minutes or until golden brown. Transfer to wire racks.

Makes about 4 dozen

Orange–Butter Icing

3 tbsp	softened butter or margarine	45 mL
$1^{1}/_{2}$ cups	confectioner's (icing) sugar, sifted	375 mL
2 tsp	orange zest	10 mL
1 tbsp	orange juice	15 mL

1. In a bowl, beat butter or margarine and sugar until smooth and creamy. Stir in orange zest and juice. Beat until smooth and the right consistency for spreading.

Sunny Lemon Yogurt Cookies

2½ cups + 2 tbsp	all-purpose flour	625 mL + 25 mL
1 tsp	baking powder	5 mL
½ tsp	baking soda	2 mL
1 tsp	salt	5 mL
2	eggs, lightly beaten	2
1½ cups	granulated sugar	375 mL
⅓ cup	vegetable oil	75 mL
½ cup	low-fat lemon yogurt	125 mL
½ tsp	finely grated lemon zest	2 mL
1 tsp	fresh lemon juice	5 mL
	Confectioner's (icing) sugar, sifted (optional)	
	Lemon-Butter Frosting (optional) (see Recipe, below)	

Preheat oven to 375°F (190°C)
Lightly greased cookie sheet

1. In a bowl, mix together flour, baking powder, baking soda and salt.

2. In another bowl, beat eggs, sugar, oil, yogurt, lemon zest and juice until well blended. Add flour mixture and mix well.

3. Drop by rounded teaspoonfuls (5 mL), about 2 inches (5 cm) apart, onto prepared cookie sheet. Bake in preheated oven for 10 to 12 minutes or until lightly browned around the edges. Cool on sheet for 2 minutes, then transfer to wire racks to cool completely. Sprinkle with confectioner's sugar or frost, if desired.

Makes about 4 dozen

HINT: When buying lemons, look for fine-textured skin. The lemon will be juicier. If there is a bit of greenish coloring, the juice will be more acidic.

Lemon-Butter Frosting

1½ cups	confectioner's (icing) sugar, sifted	375 mL
2 tbsp	softened butter or margarine	25 mL
1 tbsp	milk	15 mL
½ tsp	lemon zest	2 mL
1 tsp	lemon juice	5 mL

1. In a bowl, mix together confectioner's sugar, butter or margarine, milk, lemon zest and juice until smooth and spreadable.

Soft Raisin Cookies

1 cup	water	250 mL
2 cups	raisins	500 mL
3$\frac{1}{2}$ cups	all-purpose flour	825 mL
1 tsp	baking powder	5 mL
1 tsp	baking soda	5 mL
1 tsp	salt	5 mL
$\frac{1}{2}$ tsp	nutmeg	2 mL
$\frac{1}{2}$ tsp	cinnamon	2 mL
1 cup	softened shortening	250 mL
1$\frac{3}{4}$ cups	granulated sugar	425 mL
2	eggs	2
1 tsp	vanilla	5 mL

Preheat oven to 350°F (180°C)
Greased cookie sheet

1. In a saucepan, bring water and raisins to a boil. Cook for 3 minutes, remove from heat and let cool. Do not drain.

2. In a bowl, mix together flour, baking powder, baking soda, salt, nutmeg and cinnamon.

3. In another bowl, beat shortening and sugar until smooth and creamy. Beat in eggs, one at a time, until incorporated. Stir in vanilla. Gradually add flour mixture, blending thoroughly. Stir in raisins and liquid.

4. Drop by rounded teaspoonfuls (5 mL), about 2 inches (5 cm) apart, onto prepared cookie sheet. Bake in preheated oven for 12 to 15 minutes or until golden brown. Immediately transfer to wire racks to cool.

Makes about 6 dozen

Cinnamon Raisin Banana Cookies

2 cups	all-purpose flour	500 mL
$\frac{1}{4}$ tsp	salt	1 mL
1 tsp	cinnamon	5 mL
1 cup	raisins	250 mL
$\frac{1}{2}$ cup	chopped nuts	125 mL
$\frac{1}{2}$ cup	softened butter or margarine	125 mL
1 cup	granulated sugar	250 mL
2	eggs	2
1 cup	mashed banana	250 mL

Preheat oven to 375°F (190°C)
Lightly greased cookie sheet

1. In a bowl, mix together flour, salt, cinnamon, raisins and nuts.

2. In another bowl, beat butter or margarine and sugar until smooth and creamy. Beat in eggs, one at a time, until incorporated. Stir in banana. Add flour mixture and mix well.

3. Drop by rounded teaspoonfuls (5 mL), about 2 inches (5 cm) apart, onto prepared cookie sheet. Bake in preheated oven for 8 to 10 minutes or until golden brown. Immediately transfer to wire racks to cool.

Makes about 4 dozen

Zesty Prune Cookies

1³/₄ cups	all-purpose flour	425 mL
¹/₂ tsp	baking soda	2 mL
¹/₂ tsp	salt	2 mL
¹/₂ tsp	cinnamon	2 mL
¹/₂ tsp	nutmeg	2 mL
Pinch	ground cloves	Pinch
¹/₂ cup	softened butter or margarine	125 mL
1 cup	packed brown sugar	250 mL
1	egg	1
¹/₄ cup	milk	50 mL
1 cup	chopped dried prunes	250 mL
¹/₂ cup	chopped nuts	125 mL

Preheat oven to 400°F (200°C)
Ungreased cookie sheet

1. In a bowl, mix together flour, baking soda, salt, cinnamon, nutmeg and cloves.

2. In another bowl, beat butter or margarine and sugar until smooth and creamy. Beat in egg until well incorporated. Stir in milk. Add flour mixture and mix well. Fold in prunes and nuts.

3. Drop by rounded teaspoonfuls (5 mL), 2 inches (5 cm) apart, onto cookie sheet. Bake in preheated oven for 8 to 10 minutes or until tops spring back when lightly touched. Immediately transfer to wire racks to cool.

Makes about 4¹/₂ dozen

Diced Rhubarb Cookies

2 cups	all-purpose flour or whole wheat flour or a combination of both	500 mL
2 tsp	baking powder	10 mL
Pinch	salt	Pinch
1 tsp	cinnamon	5 mL
¹/₂ tsp	nutmeg	2 mL
¹/₂ tsp	cloves	2 mL
¹/₂ cup	softened butter	125 mL
1 cup	lightly packed brown sugar	250 mL
1	egg	1
¹/₄ cup	milk	50 mL
1 cup	diced rhubarb	250 mL
1 cup	chopped walnuts	250 mL

Preheat oven to 350°F (180°C)
Greased cookie sheet

1. In a bowl, combine flour, baking powder, salt, cinnamon, nutmeg and cloves.

2. In another bowl, beat butter and sugar until smooth and creamy. Beat in egg until well incorporated. Mix in milk. Add flour mixture and beat until smooth. Fold in rhubarb and walnuts until well combined.

3. Drop by rounded teaspoonfuls (5 mL), 2 inches (5 cm) apart, onto prepared cookie sheet. Bake in preheated oven for 18 to 20 minutes or until crisp and lightly browned. Immediately transfer to wire racks to cool.

Makes about 3¹/₂ dozen

HINT: If you are lactose intolerant, use lactose-reduced milk in baking. It can be substituted for regular milk and will not affect the results.

Hawaiian Pineapple Drops

2 cups	all-purpose flour	500 mL
1 tsp	baking powder	5 mL
1/2 tsp	baking soda	2 mL
1/4 tsp	salt	1 mL
1/2 cup	softened butter or margarine	125 mL
1 cup	lightly packed brown sugar	250 mL
1	egg	1
1 tsp	vanilla	5 mL
1 cup	crushed pineapple, well drained	250 mL

Preheat oven to 400°F (200°C)
Greased cookie sheet

1. In a bowl, mix together flour, baking powder, baking soda and salt.

2. In another bowl, beat butter or margarine and brown sugar until smooth and creamy. Beat in egg until well incorporated. Stir in vanilla. Add flour mixture and mix well. (Dough will look crumbly.) Add pineapple and mix until well blended.

3. Drop by tablespoonfuls (15 mL), 2 inches (5 cm) apart, onto prepared cookie sheet. Bake in preheated oven for 10 to 15 minutes or until golden brown. Immediately transfer to wire racks to cool.

Makes about 3 dozen

Orange Raisin Butter Cookies

1 cup	water	250 mL
2 cups	raisins	500 mL
4 cups	all-purpose flour	1 L
1 tsp	baking powder	5 mL
1 tsp	baking soda	5 mL
1 tsp	salt	5 mL
1 1/2 tsp	cinnamon	7 mL
1/4 tsp	nutmeg	1 mL
1/4 tsp	allspice	1 mL
1 cup	softened shortening or butter	250 mL
1 3/4 cups	granulated sugar	425 mL
3	eggs, beaten	3
2 tsp	vanilla	10 mL
2 tsp	grated orange zest	10 mL

HINT: To rehydrate raisins that have dried out, place in a sieve and steam over hot water for 3 to 5 minutes.

Preheat oven to 400°F (200°C)
Ungreased cookie sheet

1. In a saucepan, over medium heat, bring raisins and water to a boil. Simmer for 5 minutes. Drain, reserving liquid. Set raisins aside.

2. In a bowl, mix together flour, baking powder, baking soda, salt, cinnamon, nutmeg and allspice.

3. In another bowl, beat shortening and sugar until smooth and creamy. Beat in eggs, one at a time, until incorporated. Stir in vanilla.

4. Add flour mixture to creamed mixture alternately with reserved raisin liquid, mixing until well blended. Fold in raisins and orange zest.

5. Drop by tablespoonfuls (15 mL), 2 inches (5 cm) apart, onto cookie sheet. Using the bottom of a glass dipped in flour, flatten slightly. Bake in preheated oven for 8 to 10 minutes or until golden brown. Cool on sheet for 3 minutes, then transfer to wire racks to cool completely.

Makes about 6 dozen

Hermits

Hermits are a spicy and fruity drop cookie, originally from New England.

3¹/₂ cups	all-purpose flour	825 mL
1 tsp	baking soda	5 mL
¹/₂ tsp	salt	2 mL
1 tsp	cinnamon	5 mL
1 tsp	nutmeg	5 mL
¹/₂ cup	softened butter or margarine	125 mL
¹/₂ cup	softened shortening	125 mL
2 cups	packed brown sugar	500 mL
2	eggs	2
¹/₂ cup	cold coffee	125 mL
1 cup	chopped nuts	250 mL
1¹/₂ cups	raisins	375 mL

Preheat oven to 375°F (190°C)
Ungreased cookie sheet

1. In a bowl, sift together flour, baking soda, salt, cinnamon and nutmeg.

2. In another bowl, beat butter or margarine, shortening and brown sugar until smooth and creamy. Add eggs, one at a time, beating until incorporated. Beat in coffee. Add flour mixture and blend well. Fold in nuts and raisins.

3. Drop by rounded teaspoonfuls (5 mL), about 2 inches (5 cm) apart, onto cookie sheet. Bake in preheated oven for 8 to 10 minutes. Cool for 2 minutes on sheet, then transfer to wire racks to cool completely.

Makes about 7 dozen

Thrifty Hermit Cookies

3 cups	all-purpose flour	750 mL
2 tsp	baking powder	10 mL
¹/₄ tsp	salt	1 mL
1 tsp	allspice	5 mL
1 tsp	cinnamon	5 mL
1 tsp	nutmeg	5 mL
1 cup	softened butter or margarine	250 mL
1¹/₂ cups	granulated sugar	375 mL
1	egg	1
1 cup	chopped raisins	250 mL

Preheat oven to 375°F (190°C)
Greased cookie sheet

1. In a bowl, mix together flour, baking powder, salt, allspice, cinnamon and nutmeg.

2. In another bowl, beat butter or margarine and sugar until smooth and creamy. Beat in egg until well incorporated. Add flour mixture and mix well. Fold in raisins.

3. Drop by rounded teaspoonfuls (5 mL), about 2 inches (5 cm) apart, onto prepared cookie sheet. Bake in preheated oven for 10 to 15 minutes or until golden brown. Cool for 2 minutes, then transfer to wire racks to cool completely.

Makes about 4 dozen

Date Nut Cookies

2 cups	all-purpose flour	500 mL
1 tsp	baking soda	5 mL
1 lb	chopped dates	500 g
1 cup	softened shortening	250 mL
1 1/2 cups	lightly packed brown sugar	375 mL
2	eggs	2
2 tsp	vanilla	10 mL
1 1/4 tsp	cinnamon	6 mL
1/4 tsp	nutmeg	1 mL
1 cup	old-fashioned rolled oats	250 mL
3/4 cup	shredded coconut	175 mL
1/2 cup	chopped nuts	125 mL

Preheat oven to 375°F (190°C)
Greased cookie sheet

1. In a bowl, mix together flour and baking soda. Add dates and toss to coat.

2. In another bowl, beat shortening and brown sugar until smooth and creamy. Add eggs, one at a time, beating until well incorporated. Stir in vanilla, cinnamon and nutmeg until blended. Add oats and flour mixture, mixing until just incorporated. Fold in coconut and nuts.

3. Drop by tablespoonfuls (15 mL), about 2 inches (5 cm) apart, onto prepared cookie sheet. Bake in preheated oven for 8 to 10 minutes or until golden brown. Cool on sheet for 2 minutes, then transfer to wire racks to cool completely.

Makes about 5 dozen

Spicy Fig Drops

1/2 cup	packed dried figs	125 mL
1/2 cup	shortening	125 mL
1/4 cup	granulated sugar	50 mL
1/2 cup	molasses	125 mL
1	egg, beaten	1
1 tsp	vanilla	5 mL
1/2 tsp	lemon extract	2 mL
3 cups less 2 tbsp	all-purpose flour	750 mL less 25 mL
1 tsp	baking soda	5 mL
1/2 tsp	cinnamon	2 mL
1/4 tsp	nutmeg	1 mL
1/4 tsp	ginger	1 mL
1/4 tsp	salt	1 mL

HINT: To cut sticky foods, such as figs, prunes, dates, marshmallows and candied fruits, use kitchen scissors. Rub the blades with oil or dip them occasionally in hot water.

Preheat oven to 375°F (190°C)
Greased cookie sheet

1. In a saucepan, soak figs in boiling water for 10 minutes. Drain, cut off stems and discard. Cut figs into small pieces and set aside.

2. In a saucepan, combine shortening, sugar and molasses. Bring to a boil, remove from heat and cool to lukewarm. Beat in egg, vanilla and lemon extract.

3. In a bowl, sift together flour, baking soda, cinnamon, nutmeg, ginger and salt. Stir flour mixture into molasses mixture until well blended. Fold in reserved figs.

4. Drop by rounded teaspoonfuls (5 mL), about 2 inches (5 cm) apart, onto prepared cookie sheet. Bake in preheated oven for 12 minutes or until golden brown. Immediately transfer to wire racks to cool.

Makes about 3 dozen

Mixed Fruit 'n' Nut Drops

1 1/4 cups	all-purpose flour	300 mL
1/2 tsp	baking soda	2 mL
2 cups	quartered pitted dates	250 mL
1 cup	diced candied pineapple	250 mL
1 cup	glazed candied cherries, halved	250 mL
1/2 cup	softened butter	125 mL
1/2 cup	packed brown sugar	125 mL
1	egg	1
1 tsp	vanilla	5 mL
1/2 tsp	cinnamon	2 mL
1/2 cup	chopped walnuts	125 mL
1/2 cup	chopped pecans	125 mL
1/2 cup	chopped hazelnuts	125 mL
	Corn syrup for glaze (optional)	

Preheat oven to 350°F (180°C)
Mini baking cups or lightly greased cookie sheet

1. In a bowl, combine flour, baking soda, dates, pineapple and cherries and toss until fruit is well coated.

2. In another bowl, beat butter and brown sugar until smooth and creamy. Beat in egg until incorporated. Stir in vanilla and cinnamon. Add flour mixture and mix well. Fold in nuts.

3. Drop by rounded teaspoonfuls (5 mL), into mini baking cups placed on a cookie sheet or directly onto prepared sheet. Bake in preheated oven for 12 to 15 minutes or until tops look dry. Immediately transfer to wire racks to cool. If you prefer a glazed cookie, brush tops lightly with heated corn syrup.

Makes about 4 dozen

Orange Nut Cranberry Cookies

3 cups	all-purpose flour	750 mL
1 tsp	baking powder	5 mL
1/4 tsp	baking soda	1 mL
1/2 tsp	salt	2 mL
1/2 cup	softened butter or margarine	125 mL
1 cup	granulated sugar	250 mL
3/4 cup	packed brown sugar	175 mL
1	egg	1
1/4 cup	milk	50 mL
2 tbsp	orange juice	25 mL
2 1/2 cups	coarsely chopped frozen cranberries	625 mL
3/4 cup	chopped nuts	175 mL

Preheat oven to 375°F (190°C)
Greased cookie sheet

1. In a bowl, mix together flour, baking powder, baking soda and salt.

2. In another bowl, beat butter or margarine and sugars until smooth and creamy. Beat in egg until well incorporated. Add milk and orange juice and blend well. Add flour mixture to creamed mixture and mix well. Fold in cranberries and chopped nuts.

3. Drop by rounded teaspoonfuls (5 mL), about 2 inches (5 cm) apart, onto prepared cookie sheet. Bake in preheated oven for 10 to 15 minutes or until lightly browned. Immediately transfer to wire racks to cool

Makes about 6 dozen

Frosted Banana Split Drops

2 cups	all-purpose flour	500 mL
2 tsp	baking powder	10 mL
1/4 tsp	baking soda	1 mL
1/4 tsp	salt	1 mL
1/2 tsp	cinnamon	2 mL
1/4 tsp	ground cloves	1 mL
1 cup	packed brown sugar	250 mL
1/4 cup	softened butter or margarine	50 mL
1/4 cup	softened shortening	50 mL
2	eggs	2
1 cup	mashed bananas, about 2 to 3 medium bananas	250 mL
1/2 cup	chopped nuts	125 mL
	Chocolate or Vanilla Icing or Fresh Strawberry Frosting	

Preheat oven to 375°F (190°C)
Lightly greased cookie sheet

1. In a bowl, mix together flour, baking powder, baking soda, salt, cinnamon and ground cloves.

2. In another bowl, beat sugar, butter or margarine and shortening until smooth and creamy. Beat in eggs, one at a time, until incorporated. Blend in bananas. Add flour mixture and mix well. Fold in nuts. Cover dough and refrigerate for about 1 hour until chilled.

3. Drop by rounded teaspoonfuls (5 mL), about 2 inches (5 cm) apart, onto prepared cookie sheet. Bake in preheated oven for 8 to 10 minutes or until cookie springs back when lightly touched. Immediately transfer to wire racks to cool completely. Frost with Chocolate Icing (see recipe, page 44), Fresh Strawberry Frosting or Vanilla Icing (see Recipes, below).

Makes about 4 dozen

Fresh Strawberry Frosting

1 cup	fresh, ripe strawberries	250 mL
1/2 tsp	lemon juice	2 mL
1 1/2 cups	confectioner's (icing) sugar, sifted	375 mL

1. In a bowl, mash strawberries with a fork. Add lemon juice and mix until blended.

2. Gradually add confectioner's sugar, beating briskly with a whisk or a hand beater until fluffy. Add up to an additional 1/2 cup (125 mL) confectioner's sugar, if necessary, until mixture is the right consistency for spreading.

Vanilla Icing

1/3 cup	softened butter or margarine	75 mL
3 cups	confectioner's (icing) sugar, sifted	750 mL
1 1/2 tsp	vanilla	7 mL
2 tbsp	milk or cream	25 mL

1. In a bowl, beat butter and confectioner's sugar until smooth and blended.

2. Stir in vanilla and milk and beat until mixture is smooth and the right consistency for spreading.

Meringue Dainties

4	egg whites	4
2 tsp	vanilla	10 mL
1/2 tsp	cream of tartar	2 mL
1 cup	granulated sugar	250 mL

VARIATION

Meringue Shells
Shape batter into 3-inch (7.5-cm) mounds and bake for 1 to 1¼ hours. Remove from oven and using a spoon scoop out the soft centers. Return meringues to preheated oven 30 minutes, then transfer to wire racks. When cooled, fill centers with whipped cream or your favorite custard.

Preheat oven to 250°F (120°C)
Cookie sheet lined with greased foil

1. Beat egg whites, vanilla and cream of tartar, until soft peaks form. Beat in sugar, 2 tbsp (25 mL) at a time, until stiff peaks form.

2. Drop by rounded teaspoonfuls (5 mL), about 2 inches (5 cm) apart, onto prepared cookie sheet. Bake in preheated oven for 50 to 60 minutes or until lightly browned. Turn heat off and leave meringues to dry in oven for 30 minutes, then transfer to wire racks.

Makes about 3 dozen small meringues

Chocolate Meringue Kisses

3/4 cup	granulated sugar	175 mL
1/4 cup	cocoa	50 mL
3	egg whites	3
3/4 tsp	vanilla	4 mL
Chocolate Glaze		
3	squares (each 1 oz/28 g) semi-sweet chocolate	3
1 tbsp	shortening	15 mL

HINT: If meringues have fallen, crumble them into pieces and use in parfait dishes with whipped cream, ice cream and fruit.

Preheat oven to 300°F (150°C)
Cookie sheet lined with parchment paper or foil and sprayed with nonstick spray
Pastry bag with large star tip

1. In a bowl, mix together sugar and cocoa.

2. In another bowl, beat egg whites and vanilla until soft peaks form. Gradually beat in sugar mixture until stiff peaks form.

3. Using a pastry bag, press stars onto prepared sheet, about 2 inches (5 cm) apart. Bake in preheated oven for 30 to 35 minutes or until lightly browned. Immediately transfer to wire racks to cool.

4. To make Chocolate Glaze: In a saucepan, over low heat, melt chocolate and shortening, stirring constantly. Holding gently with your fingers, dip the top of each meringue into the glaze, then place on waxed paper to harden.

Makes about 4 dozen kisses

Brandy Lace Roll-ups

3/4 cup	all-purpose flour	175 mL
1/2 tsp	ground ginger	2 mL
1/2 cup	softened butter or margarine	125 mL
1/2 cup	corn syrup	125 mL
1/3 cup	packed brown sugar	75 mL
2 tsp	brandy or lemon juice	10 mL
1 cup	whipping cream	250 mL
1 tbsp	brandy (optional)	15 mL

HINT: For ease of rolling, bake roll-ups one cookie sheet at a time. The cookies are likely to harden before they can be rolled if you work with a larger quantity.

VARIATION

Brandy Lace Crisps
Leave cookies on cookie sheet to cool for 3 to 5 minutes, then transfer to a wire rack. Store in an airtight container away from other cookies.

Preheat oven to 375°F (190°C)
Lightly greased cookie sheet
Cake or pastry decorating bag

1. In a bowl, mix together flour and ginger.

2. In a saucepan, over medium heat, melt butter or margarine, corn syrup and brown sugar, stirring frequently. Remove from element and stir in brandy or lemon juice. Add flour mixture, mixing until well blended.

3. Drop by rounded teaspoonfuls (5 mL), about 5 inches (12.5 cm) apart, onto prepared cookie sheet. Bake in preheated oven for 6 to 8 minutes or until cookies are a rich brown and have spread into 3- to 4-inch (7.5- to 10-cm) rounds.

4. Cool for 1 to 3 minutes on sheet. Then, while still warm and working quickly, wrap each cookie around a wooden spoon handle, allowing it to firm up before sliding off. Place roll on a wire rack to cool. If cookies become too crisp to roll, return to preheated oven for about 1 minute to soften. Fill roll-ups with fresh whipped cream, flavored with brandy, if desired. Use a decorating bag with a plain or fancy tip and pipe the whipped cream into each end of the roll-up.

Makes about 2 1/2 dozen

Chocolate Jam-Filled Thumbprints

1³/₄ cups	all-purpose flour	425 mL
1 tsp	baking soda	5 mL
¹/₂ tsp	salt	2 mL
³/₄ cup	softened butter or margarine	175 mL
¹/₄ cup	granulated sugar	50 mL
¹/₂ cup	packed brown sugar	125 mL
2	eggs	2
1 tsp	vanilla	5 mL
1¹/₂ cups	mini chocolate chips	375 mL
	Raspberry jam	

HINT: To decrystalize jam, jelly or syrup, place jar in a pan of cold water, over low heat. Heat gently and the crystals will disappear.

Preheat oven to 350°F (180°C)
Greased cookie sheet

1. In a bowl, mix together flour, baking soda and salt.

2. In another bowl, cream butter or margarine and sugars until smooth and creamy. Add eggs, one at a time, beating until incorporated. Stir in vanilla. Add flour mixture and mix until just blended. Fold in chocolate chips and let stand for 10 minutes.

3. Drop by tablespoonfuls (15 mL), 2 inches (5 cm) apart, onto prepared cookie sheet. Using your thumb, a thimble or the back of a small spoon, make an indentation in each cookie. Bake in preheated oven for 10 to 12 minutes or until golden brown. Spoon raspberry jam into each indentation and transfer to wire racks to cool.

Makes about 4 dozen

Crisp Caramel Wafers

¹/₂ cup	all-purpose flour	125 mL
¹/₂ tsp	cardamom	2 mL
¹/₄ cup	sliced almonds	50 mL
3 tbsp	butter	45 mL
¹/₄ cup	corn syrup	50 mL
¹/₄ cup	packed brown sugar	50 mL
¹/₂ tsp	vanilla	2 mL

HINT: To line a cookie sheet with parchment or waxed paper, simply cut the paper to fit the sheet and place on top.

HINT: To stretch a prepared frosting and reduce its sweetness, blend a (16 oz/500 g) quantity with an 8 oz (250 g) package softened cream cheese.

Preheat oven to 350°F (180°C)
Cookie sheet lined with parchment or waxed paper

1. In a bowl, mix together flour, cardamom and almonds.

2. In a saucepan, over medium-low heat, bring butter, corn syrup and brown sugar to a boil, stirring constantly. Add vanilla and mix well. Set aside to cool slightly. Add flour mixture and stir until well blended.

3. Drop by rounded teaspoonfuls (5 mL), about 4 inches (10 cm) apart, onto prepared cookie sheet. Bake in preheated oven for 6 to 8 minutes or until golden brown. Cool on sheet for 5 minutes, then transfer to wire racks to cool completely.

Makes about 2¹/₂ dozen

Brown Sugar Cookies

3½ cups	all-purpose flour	825 mL
1 tsp	baking soda	5 mL
1 tsp	salt	5 mL
1 cup	softened shortening	250 mL
2 cups	lightly packed brown sugar	500 mL
2	eggs	2
½ cup	buttermilk	125 mL

VARIATIONS

Coconut Brown Sugar Cookies
Stir in 1 cup (250 mL) shredded coconut before chilling.

Fruit Nut Brown Sugar Cookies
Stir in 2 cups (500 mL) chopped candied fruit and 1 cup (250 mL) chopped nuts before chilling.

Preheat oven to 400°F (200°C)
Lightly greased cookie sheet

1. In a bowl, mix together flour, baking soda and salt.

2. In another bowl, beat shortening and brown sugar until smooth and creamy. Add eggs, one at a time, beating until incorporated. Beat in buttermilk. Add flour mixture and mix well. Cover dough and refrigerate for 1 hour.

3. Drop by teaspoonfuls (5 mL), about 2 inches (5 cm) apart, on prepared cookie sheet. Bake in preheated oven for 8 to 10 minutes or until cookie springs back when lightly touched. Immediately transfer to wire racks.

Makes about 6 dozen

Cinnamon Mocha Cappuccino Cookies

2 cups	all-purpose flour	500 mL
1 tsp	baking powder	5 mL
½ tsp	cinnamon	2 mL
¾ cup less 1 tbsp	softened butter or margarine	175 mL less 15 mL
1¼ cups	granulated sugar	300 mL
2	eggs	2
2 tsp	instant cappuccino or other strong coffee powder	10 mL
1 tbsp	boiling water	15 mL
⅓ cup	hot milk	75 mL
1 tsp	vanilla	5 mL
	Sugar-Cinnamon Mix (see Recipe, page 11)	
1	square (1 oz/28 g) grated semi-sweet chocolate	1

Preheat oven to 375°F (190°C)
Well-greased cookie sheet

1. In a bowl, mix together flour, baking powder and cinnamon.

2. In another bowl, beat butter or margarine and sugar until smooth and creamy. Add eggs, one at a time, beating until incorporated.

3. In a small bowl, mix together coffee, water and hot milk, stirring until coffee dissolves. Stir in vanilla and add to creamed mixture. Add flour mixture and mix thoroughly.

4. Drop by teaspoonfuls (5 mL), about 2 inches (5 cm) apart, onto prepared cookie sheet. Sprinkle tops with sugar-cinnamon mix and grated chocolate. Bake in preheated oven for 10 minutes or until bottoms are golden brown. Immediately transfer to wire racks to cool.

Makes about 2½ dozen

Cornmeal Molasses Drops

1 cup	all-purpose flour	250 mL
1 cup	yellow cornmeal	250 mL
3 tsp	baking powder	15 mL
1/2 tsp	salt	2 mL
1/3 cup	cold butter, cut into small chunks	75 mL
2 tbsp	light molasses	25 mL
6 tbsp	milk	90 mL
1/4 cup	golden raisins (optional)	50 mL

NOTE: These cookies are also delicious if allowed to cool for 5 minutes, then served warm.

Preheat oven to 425°F (220°C)
Ungreased cookie sheet

1. In a bowl, mix together flour, cornmeal, baking powder and salt. Using two knives, a pastry blender or the tips of your fingers, cut in butter until mixture resembles coarse crumbs.

2. In a measuring cup, combine molasses and milk. Add to flour mixture and mix well. Fold in raisins, if using.

3. Drop by teaspoonfuls (5 mL), about 2 inches (5 cm) apart, onto cookie sheet. Bake in preheated oven for 13 to 15 minutes or until golden brown. Immediately transfer to wire racks to cool.

Makes about 2 dozen

Herb Drop Cookies

2 1/4 cups	all-purpose flour	550 mL
2 tsp	baking soda	10 mL
1 tsp	cinnamon	5 mL
1/2 tsp	cloves	2 mL
3 tsp	ginger	15 mL
1/4 tsp	salt	1 mL
1/2 cup	softened shortening	125 mL
1/2 cup	granulated sugar	125 mL
1	egg	1
1/2 cup	molasses	125 mL
1/3 cup	strong, hot coffee	75 mL
2 tbsp	anise seeds	25 mL
2 tsp	crushed coriander seeds	10 mL
	Walnut or pecan halves (optional)	

NOTE: Vanilla Glaze: In a bowl, beat together 2 cups (500 mL) sifted confectioner's (icing) sugar, 1 tsp (5 mL) vanilla and enough milk to make the mixture spreadable.

Preheat oven to 350°F (180°C)
Greased cookie sheet

1. In a bowl, mix together flour, baking soda, cinnamon, cloves, ginger and salt.

2. In another bowl, cream shortening and sugar until smooth and creamy. Beat in egg until incorporated, then blend in molasses.

3. Add flour mixture to creamed mixture, alternately with coffee, mixing well after each addition. Stir in anise and coriander seeds.

4. Drop by rounded teaspoonfuls (5 mL), about 2 inches (5 cm) apart, onto prepared cookie sheet. Top with nuts, if desired. Bake in preheated oven for 8 to 10 minutes or until golden brown. Immediately transfer to wire racks to cool. Top with Vanilla Glaze, if desired (see note, left).

Makes about 3 1/2 dozen

Traditional Peanut Butter Cookies

Although these cookies work well as drop cookies, you can also shape them into a 1-inch (2.5-cm) ball and flatten with tines of a fork dipped in flour.

1¼ cups	all-purpose flour	425 mL
¾ tsp	baking soda	4 mL
¾ tsp	salt	4 mL
½ cup	softened shortening	125 mL
¾ cup	smooth peanut butter	175 mL
1¼ cups	firmly packed brown sugar	300 mL
1	egg	1
1 tbsp	vanilla	15 mL
3 tbsp	milk	45 mL

Preheat oven to 375°F (180°C)
Ungreased cookie sheet

1. In a bowl, mix together flour, baking soda and salt.

2. In another bowl, cream shortening, peanut butter and brown sugar until smooth. Beat in egg until incorporated. Mix in vanilla and milk until smooth. Add flour mixture and mix thoroughly.

3. Drop by rounded tablespoonfuls (15 mL), about 2 inches (5 cm) apart, onto cookie sheet. Bake in preheated oven for 6 to 8 minutes or until golden brown. Cool on sheet for 2 to 3 minutes, then transfer to wire racks to cool completely.

Makes about 3 dozen

Poppy Seed Drop Cookies

1 cup	poppy seeds	250 mL
½ cup	scalded milk	125 mL
1½ cups	all-purpose flour	375 mL
1 tsp	baking powder	5 mL
Pinch	salt	Pinch
½ tsp	cinnamon	2 mL
¼ tsp	ground cloves	1 mL
½ cup	softened butter	125 mL
½ cup	granulated sugar	125 mL
2	squares (each 1 oz/28 g) unsweetened chocolate, melted (optional) (see page 11)	2

HINT: To keep spices fresh for as long as possible, grind your own and keep in jars, sealed tightly away from heat, light and moisture. Stored this way, spices will keep for about a year.

Preheat oven to 350°F (180°C)
Greased cookie sheet

1. In a bowl, soak poppy seeds in hot milk for 30 minutes. Set aside.

2. In another bowl, mix together flour, baking powder, salt, cinnamon and cloves.

3. In a separate bowl, beat butter and sugar until smooth and creamy. Stir in chocolate, mixing until well blended. Mix in poppy seed mixture. Add flour mixture and mix thoroughly.

4. Drop by rounded teaspoonfuls (5 mL), about 2 inches (5 cm) apart, onto prepared cookie sheet. Bake in preheated oven for 20 minutes or until browned. Immediately transfer to wire racks to cool.

Makes about 2½ dozen

Classic Sour Cream Drop Cookies

2³/₄ cups	all-purpose flour	675 mL
¹/₂ tsp	baking powder	2 mL
¹/₂ tsp	baking soda	2 mL
¹/₂ tsp	salt	2 mL
¹/₂ cup	softened shortening	125 mL
1¹/₂ cups	granulated sugar	375 mL
2	eggs	2
1 tsp	vanilla	5 mL
1 cup	sour cream	250 mL

VARIATIONS

Chocolate Sour Cream Drops
Mix in 2 squares (each 1 oz/28 g) melted unsweetened chocolate to the creamed mixture, before adding flour mixture. Fold in 1 cup (250 mL) chopped nuts before chilling dough.

Fruit Cream Drops
Fold in 1 cup (250 mL) chopped dates or other candied fruit before chilling dough.

Preheat oven to 425°F (220°C)
Lightly greased cookie sheet

1. In a bowl, mix together flour, baking powder, baking soda and salt.

2. In another bowl, beat shortening and sugar until smooth and creamy. Add eggs, one at a time, beating until well incorporated. Stir in vanilla and sour cream and mix well. Gradually add flour mixture, mixing until well blended. Refrigerate dough for at least 1 hour.

3. Drop by rounded teaspoonfuls (5 mL), about 2 inches (5 cm) apart, onto prepared cookie sheet. Bake in preheated oven for 8 to 10 minutes or until lightly browned. Immediately transfer to wire racks to cool.

Makes about 5 dozen

Chocolate Icing

3	squares (each 1 oz/28 g) unsweetened chocolate	3
¹/₂ tbsp	butter	7 mL
5 tbsp	milk	75 mL
3¹/₂ cups	confectioner's (icing) sugar, sifted	825 mL
1 tsp	vanilla	5 mL

1. In the top of a double boiler, combine chocolate, butter and milk until melted and smooth.

2. Gradually beat in confectioner's sugar, then vanilla until smooth and creamy.

Almond Sugar Cookie Crisps

2 cups	all-purpose flour	500 mL
1 tsp	baking soda	5 mL
1 tsp	cream of tartar	5 mL
1 cup	softened shortening, butter-flavored, if possible	250 mL
1/2 cup	granulated sugar	125 mL
1/2 cup	packed brown sugar	125 mL
1	egg	1
1/2 tsp	vanilla	2 mL
1/2 tsp	almond extract	2 mL

HINT: To make cookies thinner and crisper, use a glass dipped in water and then sugar to press down and flatten the dough.

Preheat oven to 350°F (180°C)
Ungreased cookie sheet

1. In a bowl, mix together flour, baking soda and cream of tartar.

2. In another bowl, beat shortening and sugars until smooth and creamy. Beat in egg until well incorporated. Stir in vanilla and almond extract. Gradually add flour mixture and mix thoroughly.

3. Drop by tablespoonfuls (15 mL), about 2 inches (5 cm) apart, onto cookie sheet. Flatten with the bottom of a glass dipped in sugar. Bake in preheated oven for 10 to 12 minutes or until lightly browned. Immediately transfer to wire racks to cool. Recipe can be doubled, if desired.

Makes about 2 1/2 dozen

Whole Wheat Spice Cookies

1/4 cup	vegetable oil	50 mL
1/4 cup	molasses	50 mL
1/2 cup	granulated sugar	125 mL
1/4 cup	packed brown sugar	50 mL
2	eggs	2
1/2 cup	whole wheat flour	125 mL
1 1/2 cups	all-purpose flour	375 mL
2 tsp	baking soda	10 mL
1/4 tsp	salt	1 mL
1 tsp	ginger	5 mL
1 tsp	cinnamon	5 mL
1 tsp	cloves	5 mL

Preheat oven to 350°F (180°C)
Lightly greased cookie sheet

1. In a bowl, whisk oil, molasses, sugars and eggs until blended.

2. In a large bowl, mix together flours, baking soda, salt, ginger, cinnamon and cloves. Make a well in the center and add the molasses mixture, mixing until thoroughly blended.

3. Drop by teaspoonfuls (5 mL), about 2 inches (5 cm) apart, onto prepared cookie sheets. Bake in preheated oven for 8 to 10 minutes or until cookies are firm to the touch. Cool on sheets for 5 minutes, then transfer to wire racks to cool completely.

Makes about 3 dozen

Hand-Shaped Cookies

Hand-shaped cookies are, as their name suggests, molded into a shape by hand. The dough, which is firmer than drop cookie dough, is usually shaped into a small ball before baking. Often it is flattened slightly and imprinted with a simple pattern made by the tines of a fork or the bottom of a glass.

Nut Cookies

Fruit Cookies

Lemon Cookies

Chocolate Chip Cookies

Peanut Butter Cookies

Oatmeal Cookies

Filled Cookies

Other Hand-Shaped Cookies

Nutmeg Pecan Butter Balls

1/2 cup	softened butter	125 mL
1/3 cup	confectioner's (icing) sugar, sifted	75 mL
1/2 tsp	vanilla	2 mL
1/4 tsp	nutmeg	1 mL
Pinch	salt	Pinch
1 cup	all-purpose flour	250 mL
1/2 cup	finely chopped pecans, toasted (see page 11)	125 mL
1/2 cup	coarsely chopped pecans, toasted	125 mL

Preheat oven to 350°F (180°C)
Ungreased cookie sheet

1. In a bowl, beat butter and confectioner's sugar until smooth and creamy. Beat in vanilla, nutmeg and salt until well blended. Gradually mix in flour and toasted pecans. Wrap dough tightly in plastic wrap and refrigerate for 2 to 3 hours until firm.

2. Shape dough into 1-inch (2.5-cm) balls and roll in coarsely chopped pecans until coated. Place about 2 inches (5 cm) apart on cookie sheet. Bake in preheated oven for 12 to 15 minutes or until browned. Cool on cookie sheets for about 2 minutes, then being careful to ensure cookies don't break, transfer to wire racks to cool completely.

Makes about 2 dozen

Surprise Potato Chip Crunchies

3/4 cup	softened butter or margarine	175 mL
3/4 cup	granulated sugar	175 mL
1	egg yolk	1
1 tsp	vanilla	5 mL
1 1/2 cups	all-purpose flour	375 mL
1/3 cup	finely crushed potato chips	75 mL
1/4 cup	finely chopped nuts	50 mL
	Additional granulated sugar	

HINT: Freeze leftover raw egg whites individually in plastic ice–cube containers. Thaw for 15 to 30 minutes and use in recipes requiring egg whites only.

Preheat oven to 375°F (190°C)
Ungreased cookie sheet

1. In a bowl, beat butter and sugar until smooth and creamy. Beat in egg yolk and vanilla until well blended. Gradually add flour and mix well. Stir in potato chips and nuts.

2. Shape dough into 1-inch (2.5-cm) balls and place 2 inches (5 cm) apart on cookie sheet. For each ball, dip the bottom of a glass in sugar and flatten. Bake in preheated oven for 12 to 15 minutes or until golden brown. Leave on cookie sheet for 2 minutes to cool, then transfer to wire racks to cool completely.

Makes about 3 dozen

Cinnamon Pecan Snickerdoodles

3 cups	all-purpose flour	750 mL
1 tsp	baking powder	5 mL
1/4 tsp	salt	1 mL
1 cup	softened butter (no substitutes)	250 mL
1 1/2 cups	granulated sugar	375 mL
2	eggs	2
1 tsp	vanilla	5 mL
1/3 cup	granulated sugar	75 mL
1 tbsp	cinnamon	15 mL
1 cup	almond, pecan or walnut halves	250 mL

Preheat oven to 350°F (180°C)
Lightly greased cookie sheet

1. In a medium bowl, combine flour, baking powder and salt.

2. In another bowl, beat butter and 1 1/2 cups (375 mL) sugar until smooth and creamy. Beat in eggs, one at a time. Stir in vanilla. Add flour mixture and mix well.

3. In a small bowl, mix together 1/3 cup (75 mL) sugar and cinnamon.

4. Shape dough into 1-inch (2.5-cm) balls, then roll in cinnamon mixture to coat. Place about 2 inches (5 cm) apart on prepared cookie sheet. Press half a nut into the top of each cookie. Bake in preheated oven for 12 to 15 minutes or until golden brown. Immediately transfer to wire racks to cool.

Makes about 5 dozen

Mexican Wedding Cakes

2 cups	all-purpose flour	500 mL
1/2 cup	confectioner's (icing) sugar, sifted	125 mL
1 cup	finely chopped pecans, toasted (see page 11)	250 mL
Pinch	salt	Pinch
1 tsp	vanilla	5 mL
1 cup	cold butter, cut into 1-inch (2.5-cm) chunks (no substitutes)	500 mL
	Additional confectioner's sugar	

Preheat oven to 325°F (160°C)
Ungreased cookie sheet

1. In a bowl, mix together flour, confectioner's sugar, pecans and salt until thoroughly combined. Add vanilla and mix well.

2. Using two knives, a pastry blender or your fingers, cut butter into flour mixture until mixture resembles crumbs. Knead dough gently until it begins to hold together.

3. Shape dough into 1-inch (2.5-cm) balls and place about 2 inches (5 cm) apart on cookie sheet. Bake in preheated oven for 25 minutes until lightly browned. Immediately transfer to wire racks and cool for 5 minutes. Dip both sides of cookies in confectioner's sugar and return to racks to cool completely.

Makes about 4 dozen

HINT: To easily make chopped nuts, place pieces in a plastic bag and crush with a rolling pin. Then pour directly into a measuring cup.

Sweet Cornflake Cookies

1/2 cup	softened butter or margarine	125 mL
1/4 cup	firmly packed light brown sugar	50 mL
2 tbsp	light corn syrup	25 mL
1	egg	1
1 1/2 cups	all-purpose flour	375 mL
1 tsp	baking powder	5 mL
1/3 cup	raisins	75 mL
2 cups	honey-sweetened cornflakes, lightly crushed	500 mL

Preheat oven to 350°F (180°C)
Ungreased cookie sheet

1. In a bowl, beat butter or margarine, brown sugar and corn syrup until smooth. Add egg and beat until incorporated. Stir in flour and baking powder and mix until blended. Fold in raisins. Wrap dough tightly in plastic wrap and refrigerate about 30 minutes.

2. Shape dough into 1-inch (2.5-cm) balls, then roll in the crushed cornflakes. Place about 2 inches (5 cm) apart on cookie sheet. Flatten slightly with a fork dipped in flour. Bake in preheated oven for 15 to 18 minutes or until golden brown. Immediately transfer to wire racks to cool.

Makes about 2 to 3 dozen

Farm-Style Oatmeal Cookies

1 1/2 cups	all-purpose flour	375 mL
1 tsp	baking soda	5 mL
1 tsp	cinnamon	5 mL
1 cup	softened shortening	250 mL
1 cup	granulated sugar	250 mL
1/2 cup	lightly packed brown sugar	125 mL
1	egg, beaten	1
1 tsp	vanilla	5 mL
1 1/2 cups	quick-cooking oats	375 mL
3/4 cup	finely crushed walnuts or pecans	175 mL
	Additional granulated sugar	

Preheat oven to 350°F (180°C)
Greased cookie sheet

1. In a bowl, combine flour, baking soda and cinnamon.

2. In another bowl, beat shortening and sugars until smooth and creamy. Beat in egg and vanilla. Add flour mixture and mix well. Mix in oats and walnuts or pecans. Wrap dough tightly in plastic wrap and refrigerate for 1 hour.

3. Shape dough into 1-inch (2.5-cm) balls and place about 2 inches (5 cm) apart on prepared cookie sheet. Flatten with a fork dipped in granulated sugar. Bake in preheated oven for 10 minutes or until golden brown. Immediately transfer to wire racks to cool.

Makes about 6 dozen

Quick 'n' Easy Butter Nut Cookies

1 cup	softened butter	250 mL
6 tbsp	confectioner's (icing) sugar, sifted	90 mL
2 tsp	vanilla	10 mL
2 cups	sifted cake flour (no substitutes)	500 mL
1 cup	finely chopped nuts	250 mL
	Confectioner's (icing) sugar, sifted	

HINT: When you flatten dough with the bottom of a glass dipped in sugar, use a glass with cut designs on the bottom, so the imprint will be left as a decoration on the cookie.

Preheat oven to 350°F (180°C)
Ungreased cookie sheet

1. In a bowl, beat butter, sugar and vanilla until smooth and creamy. Gradually beat in flour until thoroughly blended. Fold in nuts. Cover and refrigerate for 30 minutes until firm.

2. Shape dough into 1-inch (2.5-cm) balls. Place about 2 inches (5 cm) apart on cookie sheet and flatten slightly with a fork or the bottom of a glass dipped in flour. Bake in preheated oven for 25 minutes or until golden brown. Immediately transfer to wire racks and sprinkle with confectioner's sugar.

Makes 3 dozen

Greek Almond Cookies

2 cups	all-purpose flour	500 mL
$^1/_2$ tsp	baking powder	2 mL
1 cup	softened butter	250 mL
$^1/_4$ cup + 2 tbsp	confectioner's (icing) sugar, sifted	50 mL + 25 mL
1	egg yolk	1
$^1/_2$ tsp	vanilla	2 mL
2 tbsp	brandy	25 mL
$^1/_2$ cup	finely chopped blanched almonds	125 mL

NOTE: A Christmas tradition in Greece is to press a whole clove into the center of each cookie before baking.

HINT: To blanch almonds, soak shelled nuts in boiling water for a few minutes. Rinse under cold water and skins will easily slip off.

Preheat oven to 325°F (160°C)
Ungreased cookie sheet

1. In a bowl, mix together flour and baking powder.

2. In another bowl, beat butter and $^1/_4$ cup (50 mL) confectioner's sugar until smooth and creamy. Add egg yolk, vanilla and brandy and beat until very light. Using a spoon, stir in almonds. Stir in flour mixture until a soft dough forms. Cover and refrigerate for 30 minutes until firm.

3. Form level tablespoonfuls (15 mL) of dough into almond shapes and place about $1^1/_2$ inches (4 cm) apart on cookie sheet. Bake in preheated oven for 25 to 30 minutes or until sandy in color. Immediately transfer to wire racks to cool.

4. Before serving or storing, sprinkle remaining 2 tbsp (25 mL) confectioner's sugar over tops of cookies.

Makes about 3 dozen

Chinese Almond Cookies

2½ cups	all-purpose flour	625 mL
1½ tsp	baking powder	7 mL
1 tsp	allspice	5 mL
½ tsp	ground cloves	2 mL
½ tsp	salt	2 mL
1 cup	softened butter or margarine	250 mL
¾ cup	granulated sugar	175 mL
1	egg	1
1 tsp	almond extract	5 mL
½ cup	finely ground slivered almonds	125 mL
1	egg yolk	1
1 tbsp	water	15 mL
32	whole blanched almonds	32

HINT: To make these cookies even in size, shape the dough into a long roll. Divide the roll in half, quarters and eighths. Divide the smallest pieces into quarters for the correct size.

Preheat oven to 350°F (180°C)
Ungreased cookie sheet

1. In a bowl, mix together flour, baking powder, allspice, cloves and salt.

2. In another bowl, beat butter or margarine and sugar until light and creamy. Beat in egg, until incorporated. Stir in almond extract. Add flour mixture and mix until blended.

3. Shape dough into 32 balls (see Hint, below) and place about 2 inches (5 cm) apart on cookie sheet. For each ball, dip the bottom of a glass in flour and flatten.

4. In a small bowl, whisk egg yolk with water. Lightly brush tops with mixture, then press an almond into the center of each cookie. Bake in preheated oven for 20 minutes or until lightly browned. Immediately transfer to wire racks to cool.

Makes 32 balls

Nutmeg Almond Balls

Using the correct amount of flour is the secret to getting these balls to maintain their shape during baking.

1 cup	softened butter	250 mL
½ cup	granulated sugar	125 mL
1 tsp	vanilla	5 mL
2 cups	all-purpose flour	500 mL
¾ cup	ground almonds, toasted (see page 11)	175 mL
1 cup	confectioner's (icing) sugar, sifted	250 mL
1 tbsp	ground nutmeg	15 mL

Preheat oven to 300°F (150°C)
Ungreased cookie sheet

1. In a bowl, beat butter and sugar until light and creamy. Stir in vanilla. Gradually add flour, mixing until blended. Fold in almonds.

2. Shape dough into 1-inch (2.5-cm) balls. Place about 2 inches (5 cm) apart on cookie sheet. Bake in preheated oven for 18 to 20 minutes or until bottoms are lightly browned. Immediately transfer to wire racks to cool completely.

3. In a bowl, mix together confectioner's sugar and nutmeg. Gently roll balls in mixture until lightly coated.

Makes about 3½ dozen

Mocha Cherry Crackles

1 cup	softened butter	250 mL
1/2 cup	granulated sugar	125 mL
1 tsp	vanilla	5 mL
1 tsp	instant coffee granules	5 mL
1/4 cup	unsweetened cocoa powder	50 mL
1/4 tsp	salt	1 mL
2 cups	all-purpose flour	500 mL
1/2 cup	finely chopped maraschino cherries	125 mL
1/2 cup	finely chopped walnuts or pecans	125 mL
	Additional granulated sugar for coating cookies	

Preheat oven to 325°F (160°C)
Ungreased cookie sheet

1. In a bowl, beat butter and sugar until smooth and creamy. Beat in vanilla, then coffee, cocoa and salt until well combined. Add flour and mix well until blended. Fold in cherries and walnuts. Wrap dough tightly in plastic wrap and refrigerate for at least 1 hour.

2. Shape dough into 1-inch (2.5-cm) balls and roll in sugar until lightly coated. Place balls about 2 inches (5 cm) apart on cookie sheet. Bake in preheated oven for 20 minutes or until tops start to crack. Immediately transfer to wire racks to cool completely.

Makes about 3 1/2 dozen

Rolled Orange Juice Balls

2 1/2 cups	all-purpose flour	625 mL
1 tbsp	baking powder	15 mL
1/2 cup	softened shortening	125 mL
1/2 cup	granulated sugar	125 mL
3	eggs	3
1 tsp	vanilla	5 mL
1/2 cup	orange juice	125 mL
	Confectioner's (icing) sugar, sifted	

HINT: If you don't need zest for a particular recipe before squeezing an orange or lemon for juice, grate the peel and freeze it for later use.

Preheat oven to 350°F (180°C)
Lightly greased cookie sheet

1. In a bowl, mix together flour and baking powder.

2. In another bowl, beat shortening and sugar until smooth and creamy. Add eggs, one at a time, beating well after each addition. Beat in vanilla. Add flour mixture, alternately with orange juice, beating constantly until a soft, sticky dough forms.

3. Scoop out dough 1 tablespoon (15 mL) at a time and roll in confectioner's sugar until it forms a ball. Place balls about 2 inches (5 cm) apart on prepared cookie sheet. Repeat with remaining dough. Bake in preheated oven for 15 minutes or until edges of cookies are lightly browned. Immediately transfer to wire racks to cool.

Makes about 3 dozen

Sugar–Cinnamon Lemon Cookies

1½ cups	all-purpose flour	375 mL
1 tsp	baking powder	5 mL
¼ tsp	salt	1 mL
1½ tsp	cinnamon	7 mL
½ tsp	grated lemon zest	2 mL
½ cup	softened butter or margarine	125 mL
1 cup	granulated sugar	250 mL
1	egg	1
1 tsp	vanilla	5 mL
	Sugar-Cinnamon Mix (see Recipe, page 11)	

Preheat oven to 350°F (180°C)
Lightly greased cookie sheet

1. In a bowl, mix together flour, baking powder, salt, cinnamon and lemon zest.

2. In another bowl, beat butter or margarine and sugar until smooth and creamy. Beat in egg until well incorporated. Stir in vanilla. Add flour mixture and mix well. Wrap tightly in plastic wrap and refrigerate for 2 hours until firm.

3. Shape dough into ¾-inch (2-cm) to 1-inch (2.5-cm) balls. Roll in sugar-cinnamon mix to coat. Place balls about 2 inches (5 cm) apart on prepared cookie sheet. Bake in preheated oven for 10 minutes or until lightly browned. Cool on sheet for 2 minutes, then transfer to wire racks to cool completely.

Makes about 3 dozen

Iced Lemon Butter Cookies

2 cups	all-purpose flour	500 mL
1 cup	confectioner's (icing) sugar, sifted	250 mL
1 tsp	baking powder	5 mL
¼ tsp	salt	1 mL
1 cup	softened butter	250 mL
1 tsp	lemon extract	5 mL
1 tsp	grated lemon zest	5 mL
1	egg	1
Lemon Butter Icing		
1 cup	confectioner's (icing) sugar, sifted	250 mL
1 tbsp	softened butter	15 mL
2½ tsp	lemon juice	12 mL

HINT: A medium-sized lemon yields about 2 to 3 tbsp (25 to 45 mL) juice and 3 tsp (15 mL) grated zest. To always have freshly squeezed juice on hand, pour into ice-cube trays and freeze. When frozen, place in plastic bags, until ready to use.

Preheat oven to 350°F (180°C)
Lightly greased cookie sheet

1. In a bowl, mix together flour, confectioner's sugar, baking powder and salt.

2. In another bowl, beat butter, lemon extract, lemon zest and egg until smooth and creamy. Add flour mixture and mix until a sticky batter forms. Wrap tightly in plastic wrap and refrigerate for at least 1 hour until firm.

3. Shape dough into 1-inch (2.5-cm) balls and place about 2 inches (5 cm) apart on prepared cookie sheet. Bake in preheated oven for 12 minutes or until cookie springs back when touched lightly. Cool for 2 minutes on cookie sheet, then transfer to a wire rack to cool completely.

4. To make Lemon Butter Icing: In a bowl, beat together confectioner's sugar, butter and lemon juice until smooth and creamy. Spread icing on tops of cookies and let harden before storing.

Makes about 2½ dozen

Lemon Thumb Cookies

2 cups	softened butter	500 mL
1½ cups	confectioner's (icing) sugar, sifted	375 mL
⅓ cup	lemon juice	75 mL
4 cups	all-purpose flour	1 L
2 cups	finely chopped walnuts or pecans	500 mL
	Assorted jams such as grape, raspberry, strawberry, apricot	

Preheat oven to 350°F (180°C)
Greased cookie sheet

1. In a bowl, cream together butter and confectioner's sugar until smooth. Beat in lemon juice until well blended. Gradually add flour and mix well. Wrap dough tightly in plastic wrap and refrigerate for 2 hours until firm.

2. Shape dough into 1-inch (2.5-cm) balls and roll in chopped nuts. Place balls about 2 inches (5 cm) apart on prepared cookie sheet. Press your thumb in the center of each ball, leaving an indentation and fill with multi-colored jams. Bake in preheated oven for 12 to 15 minutes or until golden brown. Immediately transfer to wire racks to cool.

Makes about 6 dozen

Raspberry Chocolate Chip Crackles

¼ cup	butter (no substitutes)	50 mL
1	package (10 oz/300 g) raspberry chocolate chips	1
2 cups	all-purpose flour	500 mL
2 tsp	baking powder	10 mL
¼ tsp	salt	1 mL
1½ cups	granulated sugar	375 mL
4	eggs	4
½ cup	finely chopped walnuts	125 mL
	Confectioner's (icing) sugar, sifted	

HINT: If you don't feel up to making a batch of cookies, try this easy treat. Stack four graham wafers on top of each other. Spread Chocolate Icing (see Recipe, page 44) between the wafers, over the entire top and down all sides. Set aside to allow icing to harden, then cut into three rectangular cookies.

Preheat oven to 300°F (150°C)
Greased cookie sheet

1. In the top of a double boiler, over hot water, melt butter with 1 cup (250 mL) raspberry chocolate chips, stirring until smooth. Remove from hot water and set aside.

2. In a bowl, mix together flour, baking powder and salt.

3. In another bowl, beat sugar with melted butter mixture. Add eggs, one at a time, beating until incorporated. Beat in flour mixture until well blended. Fold in walnuts and remaining raspberry chips. Wrap dough tightly in plastic wrap and refrigerate at least 1 hour.

4. Shape dough into 1-inch (2.5-cm) balls, then roll in confectioner's sugar. Place balls about 2 inches (5 cm) apart on prepared cookie sheets. Bake in preheated oven for 15 to 18 minutes or until cracked on the surface but set in the middle. Immediately transfer to wire racks to cool.

Makes about 4 dozen

Dipped Biscuit Peanut Butter Balls

³/₄ cup	smooth peanut butter	175 mL
1 can	sweetened condensed milk	1 can
1	egg	1
1 tsp	vanilla	5 mL
2 cups	biscuit mix	500 mL
6	squares (each 1 oz/28 g) semi-sweet chocolate, melted	6
4 tsp	vegetable oil	20 mL

HINT: Keep vegetable oil in a squeeze bottle for when small amounts are needed.

Preheat oven to 350°F (180°C)
Ungreased cookie sheet

1. In a bowl, beat peanut butter, condensed milk, egg and vanilla until smooth and blended. Gradually add biscuit mix and mix well. Wrap dough tightly in plastic wrap and refrigerate for 30 minutes until firm.

2. Shape dough into 1-inch (2.5-cm) balls and place about 2 inches (5 cm) apart on cookie sheet. Bake in preheated oven for 10 to 12 minutes or until lightly browned. Immediately transfer to wire racks to cool.

3. In a small bowl, mix melted chocolate with oil. Dip top half of each cookie in warm mixture and place on cookie sheet lined with waxed paper. Chill until chocolate has hardened.

Makes about 5 dozen

Crunchy Peanut Butter Cookies

1¹/₂ cups	all-purpose flour	375 mL
¹/₂ tsp	baking soda	2 mL
¹/₄ tsp	salt	1 mL
¹/₂ cup	softened butter or margarine	125 mL
¹/₂ cup	packed brown sugar	125 mL
¹/₂ cup	crunchy-style peanut butter	125 mL
1	egg	1
¹/₂ tsp	vanilla	2 mL
¹/₂ cup	chopped unsalted peanuts (optional)	125 mL

Preheat oven to 375°F (190°C)
Lightly greased cookie sheet

1. In a bowl, combine flour, baking soda and salt.

2. In another bowl, beat butter or margarine, brown sugar and peanut butter until smooth and creamy. Beat in egg and vanilla. Stir in flour mixture and mix until a stiff dough forms.

3. Shape into 1-inch (2.5-cm) balls and place about 2 inches (5 cm) apart on prepared cookie sheet. Using a fork, flatten in a criss-cross pattern. If desired, sprinkle with chopped peanuts. Bake in preheated oven for 10 minutes or until lightly browned. Immediately transfer to wire racks to cool.

Makes about 2¹/₂ dozen

The Original Dad's Cookie

1 cup	all-purpose flour	250 mL
3/4 cup	oat bran	175 mL
1 cup	quick-cooking oats	250 mL
1 tsp	baking powder	5 mL
1 tsp	baking soda	5 mL
1 1/2 tsp	cinnamon	7 mL
1 tsp	nutmeg	5 mL
1 tsp	allspice	5 mL
1 cup	softened butter or margarine	250 mL
1/4 cup	lightly packed brown sugar	50 mL
3/4 cup	granulated sugar	175 mL
2 tbsp	molasses	25 mL
1	egg	1
1 tsp	vanilla	5 mL

Preheat oven to 300°F (150°C)
Ungreased cookie sheet

1. In a bowl, mix together flour, oat bran, oats, baking powder, baking soda, cinnamon, nutmeg and allspice.

2. In another bowl, beat butter or margarine and sugars until smooth. Beat in molasses, egg and vanilla until well blended. Add flour mixture and mix well.

3. Shape dough into 1-inch (2.5-cm) balls and place about 2 inches (5 cm) apart on cookie sheet. Using the tines of a fork dipped in flour, flatten. Bake in preheated oven for 15 minutes or until golden brown. Let cool on cookie sheet for 2 to 3 minutes, then transfer to wire racks to cool completely.

Makes about 5 dozen

Coconut Oatmeal Cookies

1 1/2 cups	all-purpose flour	375 mL
1 tsp	baking powder	5 mL
1 tsp	baking soda	5 mL
1 cup	softened butter	250 mL
1 cup	granulated sugar	250 mL
1/2 cup	packed brown sugar	125 mL
2	eggs	2
1 tsp	vanilla	5 mL
1 1/2 cups	rolled oats (not instant)	375 mL
3/4 cup	shredded coconut	175 mL

Preheat oven to 350°F (180°C)
Lightly greased cookie sheet

1. In a bowl, mix together flour, baking powder and baking soda.

2. In another bowl, beat butter and sugars until smooth and creamy. Add eggs, one at a time, beating until well incorporated. Stir in vanilla. Add flour mixture and mix well. Stir in oats, then coconut, mixing until thoroughly combined.

3. Shape into 1-inch (2.5-cm) balls and place about 2 inches (5 cm) apart on prepared cookie sheet. Using the tines of a fork dipped in flour or your hand, flatten slightly. Bake in preheated oven for 8 to 10 minutes or until golden brown. Immediately transfer to wire racks to cool.

Makes about 3 dozen

Swedish Thimble Cookies

1½ cups	softened butter	375 mL
¾ cup	packed light brown sugar	175 mL
3	eggs, separated	3
3 cups	sifted all-purpose flour	750 mL
¼ tsp	salt	1 mL
2 cups	finely chopped walnuts	500 mL
	Jam or jelly	

HINT: Always buy nuts in a store where the turnover is high, as they become rancid quickly. Wrap leftover nuts well and store in the refrigerator or freezer.

Preheat oven to 300°F (150°C)
Cookie sheet lined with waxed or parchment paper

1. In a bowl, beat butter and brown sugar until smooth and creamy. Beat in egg yolks, one at a time, until well incorporated. Gradually add flour and salt, mixing until all ingredients are well combined. (Dough will be very sticky.) Wrap dough tightly in plastic wrap and refrigerate for 1 hour.

2. Beat egg whites until peaks form. Place walnuts in a small bowl.

3. Shape dough into 1-inch (2.5-cm) balls. Dip each into beaten egg whites, then roll in walnuts to coat. Place balls about 2 inches (5 cm) apart on prepared cookie sheets. Using a thimble dipped in flour, make indentations in the center of each ball. Fill with your choice of jam or jelly, using about ¼ tsp (1 mL) each, just enough to fill the indentation.

4. Bake in preheated oven for 15 to 18 minutes or until lightly browned. Allow to cool on cookie sheet for 2 to 3 minutes, then transfer to wire racks to cool completely.

Makes about 5 dozen

Chocolate Cherry Thumbprint Cookies

1 1/2 cups	all-purpose flour	375 mL
1/2 cup	cocoa	125 mL
1/4 tsp	baking powder	1 mL
1/4 tsp	baking soda	1 mL
1/2 cup	softened butter	125 mL
1 cup	granulated sugar	250 mL
1	egg	1
1 1/2 tsp	vanilla	7 mL
1	jar (10 oz/284 mL) maraschino cherries	1
4 tsp	reserved cherry juice	20 mL
3/4 cup	mini chocolate chips	175 mL
1/2 cup	condensed milk	125 mL

Preheat oven to 350°F (180°C)
Ungreased cookie sheet

1. In a bowl, sift together flour, cocoa, baking powder and baking soda.

2. In another bowl, beat butter and sugar until smooth and creamy. Beat in egg, then vanilla until well incorporated. Mix in flour mixture until well blended.

3. Shape dough into 1-inch (2.5-cm) balls and place about 2 inches (5 cm) apart on cookie sheet. With your thumb, make an indentation in the center of each ball. Drain cherries and save the juice. Place a cherry in the center of each ball.

4. In a small saucepan, melt chocolate chips and condensed milk, stirring until mixture is smooth. Add cherry juice and mix well. Spoon 1 tsp (5 mL) of mixture over top of cookies, covering the cherry. Bake in preheated oven for 10 to 12 minutes or until golden brown. Transfer to wire racks to cool.

Makes about 4 dozen

A Honey of a Cookie

3 1/2 cups	all-purpose flour	825 mL
2 tsp	baking soda	10 mL
1 cup	softened butter or margarine	250 mL
1 cup	packed brown sugar	250 mL
2	eggs	2
6 tbsp	liquid honey	90 mL
1 tsp	vanilla	5 mL

HINT: When measuring spoonfuls of honey or molasses, coating the spoon lightly with oil helps the sticky ingredient to slide off and makes clean-up easier.

Preheat oven to 350°F (180°C)
Ungreased cookie sheet

1. In a bowl, mix together flour and baking soda.

2. In another bowl, beat butter and brown sugar until smooth and creamy. Add eggs, one at a time, beating until well incorporated. Beat in honey and vanilla until smooth. Add flour mixture and mix well. (Dough will be very thick.) Wrap dough tightly in plastic wrap and refrigerate until firm, at least 1 hour.

3. Shape dough into 1-inch (2.5-cm) balls and place about 2 inches (5 cm) apart on cookie sheet. Bake in preheated oven for 10 to 15 minutes or until golden brown. Immediately transfer to wire racks to cool.

Makes about 4 dozen

Sesame Seed Cookies

1½ cups	whole wheat flour	375 mL
1 tsp	baking powder	5 mL
¼ tsp	salt	1 mL
¼ cup	softened butter or margarine	50 mL
¼ cup	liquid honey	50 mL
¼ cup	sesame paste (tahini)	50 mL
½ tsp	almond extract	2 mL
½ cup	sesame seeds, toasted (see page 11)	125 mL

HINT: When a recipe calls for room-temperature or softened butter grate cold butter. It will soften very quickly.

Preheat oven to 350°F (180°C)
Lightly greased cookie sheet

1. In a bowl, mix together flour, baking powder and salt.

2. In another bowl, beat butter or margarine, honey, sesame paste and almond extract until smooth. Add flour mixture and mix well. Stir in sesame seeds.

3. Shape dough into 1-inch (2.5-cm) balls and place about 2 inches (5 cm) apart on prepared cookie sheet. Using the tines of a fork dipped in flour, flatten, or using your hands, mold into crescent shapes. (Wet your hands first, if using to mold the dough.) Bake in preheated oven for 10 to 12 minutes or until lightly browned. Immediately transfer to wire racks to cool.

Makes about 2 dozen

Chinese Chews

¼ cup	softened butter or margarine	50 mL
2	eggs	2
1 tsp	vanilla	5 mL
½ cup	liquid honey	125 mL
½ cup	lightly toasted sesame seeds, divided (see Note, below)	125 mL
¼ cup	chopped raisins	50 mL
1 cup	chopped dates	250 mL
½ cup	chopped walnuts	125 mL
¾ cup	whole wheat or all-purpose flour	175 mL
	Confectioner's (icing) sugar, sifted (optional)	

NOTE: If you prefer a sweeter cookie, use only ¼ cup (50 mL) sesame seeds and roll the cookies in ¼ cup (50 mL) confectioner's sugar.

Preheat oven to 350°F (180°C)
Greased 8-inch (2-L) square baking pan

1. In a bowl, beat butter or margarine, eggs, vanilla and honey until light and fluffy.

2. Stir in ¼ cup (50 mL) sesame seeds, raisins, dates and walnuts and mix well. Gradually add flour, mixing until thoroughly blended.

3. Using your hands spread batter into prepared pan. Bake in preheated oven for 20 minutes, until set. Remove from oven and cut into fingers, about 2x1½ inches (5x4 cm). Using a lifter or a knife, lift out fingers. Cool very slightly, then shape into balls in the palm of your hands. On a plate, roll in remaining sesame seeds, then confectioner's sugar, if desired, until well coated. Cool on wire racks.

Makes about 2 dozen

Old-Fashioned Spice Balls

3 cups	all-purpose flour	750 mL
2 cups	granulated sugar	500 mL
4 tsp	baking soda	20 mL
1 tsp	salt	5 mL
1 tsp	cinnamon	5 mL
1 tsp	allspice	5 mL
1 tsp	ginger	5 mL
2¹/₂ cups	old-fashioned rolled oats	625 mL
²/₃ cup	softened shortening	160 mL
¹/₂ cup	butter or margarine	125 mL
2	eggs, lightly beaten	2
¹/₂ cup	warm corn syrup	125 mL

Preheat oven to 350°F (180°C)
Cookie sheet lined with parchment or waxed paper

1. In a bowl, mix together flour, sugar, baking soda, salt, cinnamon, allspice, ginger and rolled oats.

2. Using two knives, a pastry blender or your fingers, cut in shortening and butter until mixture resembles coarse crumbs. Add eggs and warm syrup (be sure it is warm or dough will not be firm enough) and mix well.

3. Shape dough into 1-inch (2.5-cm) balls and place about 2 inches (5 cm) apart on prepared cookie sheet. Bake in preheated oven for 10 to 12 minutes or until golden brown. Immediately transfer to wire racks to cool.

Makes about 6 dozen

Ginger Snaps

2 cups	all-purpose flour	500 mL
3 tsp	baking soda	15 mL
¹/₄ tsp	salt	1 mL
1 tsp	cinnamon	5 mL
1 tsp	ginger	5 mL
¹/₂ tsp	ground cloves	2 mL
³/₄ cup	softened shortening	175 mL
1 cup	granulated sugar	250 mL
1	egg	1
¹/₄ cup	molasses	50 mL
	Granulated sugar	

Preheat oven to 350°F (180°C)
Greased cookie sheet

1. In a bowl, mix together flour, baking soda, salt, cinnamon, ginger and cloves.

2. In another bowl, beat shortening and sugar until smooth and creamy. Add egg and beat until well incorporated. Mix in molasses until well blended. Add flour mixture and stir well.

3. Shape dough into 1-inch (2.5-cm) to ³/₄-inch (2-cm) balls, then roll in granulated sugar. Place on prepared cookie sheet about 2 inches (5 cm) apart. Bake in preheated oven for 10 to 12 minutes, depending upon size of balls. Immediately transfer to wire racks to cool.

Makes 5 to 6 dozen

Crispy Cheddar Cookies

1 cup	all-purpose flour	250 mL
$^1/_2$ cup	butter	125 mL
$1^1/_2$ cups	shredded old Cheddar cheese	375 mL
1 cup	crisp rice cereal	250 mL
1	beaten egg	1

Preheat oven to 350°F (180°C)
Ungreased cookie sheet

1. In a bowl, using two knives, a pastry blender or your fingers, combine flour and butter until mixture resembles coarse crumbs. Add cheese, cereal and egg and mix until well blended.

2. Shape dough into either 1-inch (2.5-cm) or $^3/_4$-inch (2-cm) balls and place 2 inches (5 cm) apart on cookie sheet. Flatten slightly with a fork. Bake in preheated oven for 15 to 17 minutes, depending upon size of balls, until golden brown. Immediately transfer to wire racks to cool.

Makes about 4 dozen smaller and $2^1/_2$ dozen larger cookies

Wholesome Cheddar Bran Cookies

$1^3/_4$ cups	all-purpose flour	425 mL
$^1/_2$ tsp	baking powder	2 mL
$^1/_2$ tsp	baking soda	2 mL
$^1/_2$ tsp	salt	2 mL
$^3/_4$ cup	softened butter or margarine	175 mL
1 cup	lightly packed brown sugar	250 mL
1	egg	1
1 tsp	vanilla	5 mL
3 cups	crushed bran flakes cereal	750 mL
$^1/_2$ cup	shredded Cheddar cheese	125 mL
$^1/_2$ cup	raisins	125 mL
$^1/_2$ cup	chopped pecans or other nuts	125 mL

Preheat oven to 350°F (180°C)
Ungreased cookie sheet

1. In a bowl, mix together flour, baking powder, baking soda and salt.

2. In another bowl, beat butter or margarine and sugar until smooth and creamy. Beat in egg, then vanilla. Add flour mixture and mix well. Stir in bran flakes, cheese, raisins and nuts until mixture is crumbly.

3. Shape dough into 1-inch (2.5-cm) balls. Place about 2 inches (5 cm) apart on cookie sheet. Bake in preheated oven for 15 to 18 minutes or until lightly browned. Cool on cookie sheet for 3 to 5 minutes, then transfer to wire racks to cool completely.

Makes about 6 dozen

HINT: Before you grate cheese, spray the grater with non-stick cooking spray to ease clean up.

Cut Cookies

Although cut cookies are the most fun to make, they are a bit trickier than drop or hand-shaped cookies because the dough must be the right consistency to roll. If it is too wet, it will stick to the rolling pin and if it is too dry it will crack. To make it easier to handle, the dough must be chilled, usually for at least an hour and often as long as overnight. If desired, you can wrap the dough tightly in plastic wrap and refrigerate for up to a week. When you're ready to bake, roll the dough out, thinly, and cut your cookies as close together as possible.

The Ultimate Sugar Cookie

This is the classic cut cookie. For an extra special version, add lemon and almond extract along with the vanilla.

2 cups	all-purpose flour	500 mL
1 1/2 tsp	baking powder	7 mL
1/2 tsp	salt	2 mL
1 cup	granulated sugar	250 mL
1/2 cup	softened butter	125 mL
1	egg	1
1 tsp	vanilla	5 mL
1/4 tsp	each lemon and almond extract (optional)	1 mL
1 tbsp	milk or cream	15 mL
	Granulated or tinted sugar for sprinkling	

Preheat oven to 375°F (190°C)
Ungreased cookie sheet
Cookie cutters

1. In a bowl, sift together flour, baking powder and salt.

2. In another bowl, cream sugar and butter until smooth. Beat in egg until well incorporated. Stir in vanilla, almond extract and lemon extract, if using, and milk or cream. Gradually add flour mixture and mix until dough is firm enough to handle. Wrap in plastic wrap and refrigerate for 1 hour.

3. On a lightly floured surface, roll dough out to 1/8-inch (0.25-cm) thickness. Using cookie cutters or a glass dipped in flour, cut out desired shapes. Place about 2 inches (5 cm) apart on cookie sheets and sprinkle with sugar. Bake in preheated oven for 8 to 10 minutes until lightly browned. Immediately transfer to wire racks to cool.

Makes about 50 small cookies

VARIATIONS

Sour Cream Cookies
Sift 1/4 tsp (1 mL) nutmeg and 1/4 tsp (1 mL) baking soda with the flour. Reduce baking powder to 1/2 tsp (2 mL). Substitute 1/2 tsp (2 mL) lemon extract for the vanilla. Substitute 1/3 cup (75 mL) sour cream for the milk.

Lemon Sugar Cookies
Substitute 1 tsp (5 mL) lemon extract and 2 tsp (10 mL) grated lemon zest for the vanilla.

Chocolate Sugar Cookies
Add 2 squares (each 1 oz/28 g) melted unsweetened chocolate after the egg. If desired, add 1 cup (250 mL) finely chopped nuts to the flour mixture.

Shaped Sugar Cookies
Add 1/3 cup (75 mL) chopped almonds and the grated zest of 1/2 lemon to the flour mixture. Shape into 1-inch (2.5-cm) balls and flatten with a fork.

Wholesome Banana Granola Drops (page 16)
Hermits (page 34)
Traditional Peanut Butter Cookies (page 43)
Baba Mary's Thimble Cookies (page 146)

Dad's Favorite Chocolate
Chip Cookies (page 26)

Golden Coconut
Macaroons (page 28)

Mexican Wedding Cakes (page 49)

Chinese Chews (page 60)
Esther's Famous Komish
Bread Cookies (page 140)

Jam Crescents (page 72)
Easy Elephant Ears (page 74)

The Refrigerator Cookie (page 74)

Apricot Almond Biscotti (page 88)

Sugar, Spice 'n' Everything Nice Cookies

2 cups + 2 tbsp	all-purpose flour	500 mL + 25 mL
3/4 tsp	cinnamon	4 mL
1 tsp	cardamom	5 mL
1 tsp	ground ginger	5 mL
Pinch	freshly ground black pepper	Pinch
1 cup	softened butter	250 mL
1/2 cup + 2 tbsp	packed brown sugar	125 mL + 25 mL
2 tsp	lemon zest	10 mL

Preheat oven to 325°F (160°C)
Cookie sheet lined with parchment or waxed paper
Cookie cutters

1. In a bowl, sift together flour, cinnamon, cardamom, ginger and black pepper.

2. In another bowl, beat butter and sugar until smooth. Stir in lemon zest. Gradually add flour mixture until a soft dough forms. Shape dough into two flattened disks, wrap tightly in plastic wrap and refrigerate for 1 to 2 hours until firm.

3. Place one at a time between two sheets of waxed paper and roll out to $1/4$-inch (0.5-cm) thickness. Using cookie cutters or glass dipped in flour, cut out desired shapes. Place about 2 inches (5 cm) apart on prepared cookie sheet. Bake in preheated oven for 8 to 10 minutes until golden brown. Transfer to wire racks.

Makes about 3 dozen

Ginger Spice Snaps

4 cups	all-purpose flour	1 L
1 tsp	baking soda	5 mL
1 1/2 tsp	salt	7 mL
1/2 tsp	nutmeg	2 mL
1/4 tsp	allspice	1 mL
1/2 tsp	cloves	2 mL
1 1/2 tsp	ginger	7 mL
1/2 cup	softened shortening	125 mL
1 cup	granulated sugar	250 mL
1/2 cup	water	125 mL
1 cup	dark molasses sugar	250 mL
	Granulated sugar for sprinkling	

HINT: To measure solid shortening, line a measuring cup with plastic wrap and fill it with shortening. It lifts out easily and the cup stays clean.

Preheat oven to 375°F (190°C)
Well-greased cookie sheet
Cookie cutters

1. In a bowl, mix together flour, baking soda, salt, nutmeg, allspice, cloves and ginger.

2. In another bowl, cream shortening and sugar until smooth. Add water and molasses and mix well. Stir in flour mixture and mix until well blended and a soft dough forms. Wrap dough tightly in plastic wrap and refrigerate for at least 3 hours.

3. On a lightly floured surface, roll dough out to $1/4$-inch (0.5-cm) thickness. Using cookie cutters or glass dipped in flour, cut into 3-inch (7.5-cm) circles. Sprinkle with sugar and place about 2 inches (5 cm) apart on prepared cookie sheet. Bake in preheated oven for 10 to 12 minutes until browned. Cool on sheets for 5 minutes, then transfer to wire racks.

Makes about 4 dozen

Little Gingerbread People

2 cups	all-purpose flour	500 mL
1 tsp	baking powder	5 mL
1 tsp	baking soda	5 mL
1 tsp	cinnamon	5 mL
1 tsp	allspice	5 mL
1 1/2 tsp	ground ginger	7 mL
1/2 cup	softened butter	125 mL
1/2 cup	granulated sugar	125 mL
1/2 cup	molasses or dark corn syrup	125 mL
1	egg yolk	1
	Colored icings and candies for decoration	

Preheat oven to 350°F (180°C)
Ungreased cookie sheet
Gingerbread children cookie cutters

1. In a bowl, mix together flour, baking powder, baking soda, cinnamon, allspice and ginger.

2. In another bowl, beat butter and sugar until smooth and creamy. Beat in molasses or corn syrup (mixture will look curdled) and then egg yolk until incorporated. Gradually add flour mixture, beating well. (Dough will be sticky.) Divide dough into four and shape into flattened disks. Wrap tightly in plastic wrap and refrigerate for 3 hours until firm.

3. On a floured surface, roll dough out to 1/4-inch (0.5-cm) thickness and cut out figures. Place about 2 inch (5 cm) apart on cookie sheets. Bake in preheated oven for 6 to 8 minutes until slightly firm. Cool on sheets for 5 minutes, then transfer to wire racks. Decorate cookies with colored icings and candies, as desired.

Makes about 2 1/2 dozen

Nurnbergers

These delicious honey-spice cookies get their unusual name from the Bavarian city of Nurnberg where they originated.

2³/₄ cups	all-purpose flour	675 mL
¹/₂ tsp	baking soda	2 mL
1 tsp	cinnamon	5 mL
¹/₂ tsp	nutmeg	2 mL
¹/₂ tsp	allspice	2 mL
¹/₄ tsp	cloves	1 mL
¹/₃ cup	cut-up citron (see Note, below)	75 mL
¹/₂ cup	chopped nuts	125 mL
1 cup	liquid honey	250 mL
³/₄ cup	packed brown sugar	175 mL
1	egg	1
1 tsp	grated lemon zest	5 mL
1 tbsp	lemon juice	15 mL
	Blanched almond halves	
	Candied cherries	

Sugar Glaze

1 cup	granulated sugar	250 mL
¹/₂ cup	water	125 mL

NOTE: Citron is a semi-tropical fruit that looks like a huge lemon. It can be purchased as candied citron especially for baking in specialty stores and supermarkets.

Preheat oven to 400°F (200°C)
Lightly greased cookie sheet
Cookie cutters

1. In a bowl, mix together flour, baking soda, cinnamon, nutmeg, allspice, cloves, citron and nuts.

2. In a small saucepan, heat honey to boiling. Remove from heat and pour into a large bowl to cool thoroughly.

3. Add brown sugar, egg, lemon zest and juice to honey and mix well. Stir in flour mixture and mix until dough forms. Cover and refrigerate for at least 4 hours or preferably overnight.

4. Divide dough into four portions and return three to refrigerator. On a lightly floured surface, roll the first portion to ¹/₄-inch (0.5-cm) thickness. Using cookie cutters or a glass dipped in flour, cut into 2-inch (5-cm) rounds, and place on prepared cookie sheet. Press 5 almond halves, end to end, around the edge of the circle to form a rim and press a candied cherry in the center. Repeat with remaining dough.

5. Bake in preheated oven for 10 to 12 minutes or until cookie springs back when touched lightly with finger. Immediately transfer to wire racks to cool.

6. To make Sugar Glaze: In a small bowl, beat sugar and water. While cookies are still hot, brush tops lightly.

Makes about 5 dozen

Maple Syrup Cookies

3¹/₂ cups	all-purpose flour	825 mL
2 tsp	baking powder	10 mL
¹/₂ tsp	salt	2 mL
1 cup	softened butter	250 mL
1 cup	firmly packed brown sugar	250 mL
2	eggs	2
1 tsp	vanilla	5 mL
¹/₃ cup	pure maple syrup	75 mL

HINT: For optimum results, bake cookies one sheet at a time. If you do bake two sheets at the same time, place one on the middle rack of your oven and the other on the next lowest rung. Baking two sheets next to each other affects the heat flow and produces underbaked cookies.

Preheat oven to 350°F (180°C)
Greased cookie sheet
Cookie cutters

1. In a bowl, combine flour, baking powder and salt.

2. In another bowl, beat butter and brown sugar until smooth and creamy. Beat in eggs, one at a time, until incorporated. Mix in vanilla and syrup. Add flour mixture in three batches, beating well after each addition. Wrap tightly in plastic wrap and refrigerate at least 4 hours.

3. Divide dough into four portions. Place between two sheets of waxed paper. Roll out, one portion at a time, to ¹/₈-inch (0.25-cm) thickness. Using cookie cutters or a glass dipped in flour, cut into desired shapes. Place about 2 inches (5 cm) apart on prepared sheet. Bake in preheated oven for 8 to 10 minutes or until edges are golden brown. Immediately transfer to wire racks.

Makes about 6 dozen

Danish Jam Squares

2 cups	all-purpose flour	500 mL
1 tbsp	granulated sugar	15 mL
3¹/₂ tsp	baking powder	17 mL
¹/₂ tsp	salt	2 mL
5 tbsp	shortening	60 mL
³/₄ cup	milk	175 mL
	Jam or jelly of your choice	

HINT: Whenever cookie dough is too sticky to work with, chilling it in the refrigerator for about 20 minutes will firm it up to the right consistency.

Preheat oven to 350°F (180°C)
Lightly greased cookie sheet

1. In a bowl, mix together flour, sugar, baking powder and salt.

2. Using two knives, a pastry blender or your fingers, work in shortening until mixture resembles coarse crumbs. Gradually stir in enough milk to make a soft dough.

3. On a lightly floured surface, knead dough lightly. Roll into a square about ¹/₈-inch (0.25-cm) thick and cut into 2¹/₂-inch (6-cm) squares. Place 1 tsp (5 mL) jam or jelly in the center of each. Bring the four corners to the center and pinch together, making a small square envelope. Place about 2 inches (5 cm) apart on prepared cookie sheet. Bake in preheated oven for 15 to 20 minutes until golden brown. Transfer to wire racks lined with waxed paper.

Makes about 2¹/₂ dozen

Cinnamon Sugar Diamonds

1²/₃ cups	all-purpose flour	410 mL
¹/₂ tsp	baking powder	2 mL
¹/₄ tsp	salt	1 mL
¹/₂ cup	softened butter or margarine	125 mL
1 cup	granulated sugar	250 mL
2	egg yolks	2
1 tsp	vanilla	5 mL
1 tbsp	whipping cream plus additional for glazing cookies	1 tbsp
1 tbsp	granulated sugar	15 mL
1 tsp	cinnamon	5 mL

HINT: To ease clean-up when making cut-out cookies, place a piece of plastic wrap loosely over the rolled dough. Using your cookie cutter, press down on the plastic wrap until your shape is cut. Your cookie cutter stays clean because the plastic wrap is between it and the dough.

Preheat oven to 375°F (190°C)
Greased cookie sheet

1. In a bowl, mix together flour, baking powder and salt.

2. In another bowl, beat butter or margarine and sugar until smooth and creamy. Beat in egg yolks until well incorporated. Stir in vanilla and 1 tbsp (15 mL) whipping cream. Add flour mixture and mix well. Cover and refrigerate for several hours or overnight.

3. In a bowl, mix together sugar and cinnamon. Set aside.

4. On a lightly floured surface, divide dough into three portions. Roll out one portion at a time to ¹/₈-inch (0.25-cm) thickness. Cut dough into diamond shapes, 3 inches (7.5 cm) long and 1¹/₂ inches (4 cm) at widest point. Place about 2 inches (5 cm) apart on prepared cookie sheet. Brush tops with additional whipping cream, then with sugar-cinnamon mixture. Bake in preheated oven for 5 to 6 minutes until lightly browned. Cool slightly and then transfer to wire racks to cool completely.

Makes about 6 dozen

Apricot Cream Cheese Kolacky

These sweet treats are part of both the Polish and Czech cultures. Often filled with poppy seeds or nuts, they're filled with fruit preserves and cream cheese here.

2 cups	all-purpose flour	500 mL
2 tbsp	granulated sugar	25 mL
2 tsp	baking powder	10 mL
1/2 tsp	salt	2 mL
1 cup	softened butter or margarine	250 mL
1 cup + 2 tbsp	softened cream cheese	250 mL + 25 mL
2	eggs	2
1/2 cup	apricot or cherry preserves	125 mL

Preheat oven to 375°F (190°C)
Ungreased cookie sheet
Cookie cutters

1. In a bowl, mix together flour, sugar, baking powder and salt.

2. In another bowl, beat butter and cream cheese until smooth. Beat in eggs, one at a time, until incorporated. Gradually add flour mixture, mixing until a stiff dough forms. Cover and refrigerate for 3 hours.

3. On a lightly floured surface, divide dough into four portions. Roll each portion to 1/4-inch (5-cm) thickness. Using a cookie cutter or a glass dipped in flour, cut into circles. Dip your index finger in flour and make a deep indentation in the center of each round. Fill with a scant 1/4 tsp (1 mL) preserves. (Do not use too much as the fruit will spill over.) Place rounds about 2 inches (5 cm) apart on cookie sheet. Bake in preheated oven for about 15 minutes until golden brown. Immediately transfer to wire racks.

Makes about 6 dozen

Apricot Bundles

1 1/4 cups	all-purpose flour	300 mL
1/2 tsp	baking powder	2 mL
1/4 tsp	salt	1 mL
3 tbsp	softened butter	45 mL
3 tbsp	softened margarine	45 mL
1/2 cup	granulated sugar	125 mL
1	egg	1
2 tsp	grated orange zest	10 mL
1/2 tsp	vanilla	2 mL
Apricot Filling		
1/2 cup	chopped dried apricots	125 mL
1/3 cup	orange juice	75 mL
2 tbsp	light brown sugar	25 mL
	Confectioner's (icing) sugar, sifted	

Preheat oven to 350°F (180°C)
Lightly greased cookie sheet

1. In a bowl, mix together flour, baking powder and salt.

2. In another bowl, beat butter, margarine and sugar until smooth and creamy. Beat in egg, orange zest and vanilla until well blended. Add flour mixture and mix until a soft dough forms. Wrap tightly in plastic wrap and refrigerate for at least 2 hours.

3. To make Apricot Filling: In a small saucepan, bring apricots, orange juice and brown sugar to a boil. Lower heat, cover and simmer for about 10 minutes until apricots are soft. Allow to cool, then purée in food processor. If mixture is too thick, add a little orange juice.

4. On a lightly floured surface, divide dough into three portions. Roll each portion into a 6-inch (15-cm) square and cut into nine 2-inch (5-cm) squares. In a narrow diagonal line, spread a level teaspoonful (5 cm) of filling across each square diagonally, from one corner to the opposite corner. Fold the other two opposite corners together to make a triangle. Using your fingers or the tines of a fork, press to seal. Repeat with each piece of dough.

5. Place bundles about 2 inches (5 cm) apart on prepared cookie sheet. Bake in preheated oven for 10 to 12 minutes. Immediately transfer to wire racks to cool, then sprinkle with confectioner's sugar.

Makes about 2 dozen

Jam Crescents

3¹/₄ cups	all-purpose flour	800 mL
¹/₂ tsp	baking powder	2 mL
¹/₂ tsp	salt	2 mL
1	envelope (¹/₃ oz/9 g) vanilla sugar	1
1 cup	softened butter	250 mL
¹/₄ cup	softened margarine or shortening	50 mL
3	egg yolks	3
1 cup	sour cream	250 mL
	Plum or seedless raspberry jam	
	Granulated sugar	

Preheat oven to 350°F (180°C)
Ungreased cookie sheet

1. In a bowl, combine flour, baking powder, salt and vanilla sugar.

2. In another bowl, beat butter, margarine or shortening, egg yolks and sour cream until well blended. Add dry ingredients and beat until a soft dough forms. (If dough is sticky, transfer to a lightly floured board and knead in additional flour until right consistency is achieved.) Form dough into a large ball, then cut in half. Flatten each half into a disk and wrap tightly in plastic wrap. Refrigerate at least 2 hours until dough is firm.

3. On a lightly floured surface, divide dough into 10 balls. Return nine to the refrigerator until ready to use and roll one ball into an 8-inch (20-cm) circle. Using a knife or a pastry cutter, fluted, if desired, cut into eight pie-shaped wedges.

4. Spread about ¹/₂ tsp (2 mL) jam on outer edge of each wedge. Beginning with the outer edge and finishing with the point in the center, roll up to form crescents. Sprinkle generously with sugar and shake off excess. Place, point side down, about 2 inches (5 cm) apart on cookie sheet. Repeat with remaining dough.

5. Bake in preheated oven for 15 to 17 minutes until bottom of crescents are golden brown. Immediately transfer to wire racks to cool.

Makes about 6¹/₂ dozen

Sliced Cookies

Often called refrigerator cookies, sliced cookies are among the easiest and most convenient cookies to make. You can mix the dough, shape it into a roll, wrap tightly in plastic wrap and refrigerate for as long as a week. When you're ready to bake, slice off pieces of dough — only as much as you want — and bake. You can always have warm cookies ready and waiting — even for unexpected guests.

Easy Elephant Ears

	Granulated sugar	
¹/₂ lb	frozen puff pastry, defrosted	250 g

VARIATION

Cinnamon Nut Elephant Ears
In a food processor with a metal blade, process ¹/₂ cup (125 mL) chopped nuts, 2 tbsp (25 mL) granulated sugar and ¹/₂ tsp (2 mL) cinnamon until finely ground. Sprinkle dough with mixture before folding.

Preheat oven to 425°F (220°C)
Ungreased cookie sheet

1. Sprinkle a pastry board with a thick layer of sugar. Place puff pastry on top and roll into a neat oblong.
2. Fold one long side of puff pastry inward, like a jellyroll, but stopping at the center. Repeat on the other side, so the two rolls meet in the center. Cut into slices ¹/₄ inch (0.5 cm) thick and press each slice in sugar.
3. Place slices on cookie sheet. Bake in preheated oven for 6 to 8 minutes. Turn over and bake for another 6 to 8 minutes until golden brown.

Makes about 1 dozen

The Refrigerator Cookie

2 cups	all-purpose flour	500 mL
2 tsp	baking powder	10 mL
¹/₂ tsp	salt	2 mL
¹/₂ cup	softened shortening	125 mL
³/₄ cup	granulated sugar	175 mL
¹/₂ cup	packed brown sugar	125 mL
1	egg	1
1 tsp	vanilla	5 mL
¹/₂ cup	chopped nuts	125 mL

VARIATIONS

Chocolate Refrigerator Cookies
Add 2 squares (each 1 oz/28 g) melted chocolate or 4 tbsp (50 mL) cocoa along with the vanilla.

Coconut Refrigerator Cookies
Substitute ¹/₂ cup (125 mL) flaked or shredded coconut for the nuts.

Spice Refrigerator Cookies
Add 1 tsp (5 mL) each of cinnamon, ginger and nutmeg to the dry ingredients.

Preheat oven to 425°F (220°C)
Lightly greased cookie sheet

1. In a bowl, mix together flour, baking powder and salt.
2. In another bowl, beat shortening and sugars until smooth and creamy. Beat in egg until well incorporated. Stir in vanilla and nuts. Add flour mixture and mix until a soft dough forms.
3. On a lightly floured surface, divide dough in half. Shape into two long rolls about 2 inches (5 cm) wide. Wrap each tightly in plastic wrap and refrigerate for at least 2 hours until firm.
4. When ready to bake, remove from wrap and cut dough into slices ¹/₄ inch (0.5 cm) thick. Place about 2 inches (5 cm) apart on prepared cookie sheet. Bake in preheated oven for 8 to 10 minutes until golden brown. Immediately transfer to wire racks to cool.

Makes about 4 dozen

Easy Icebox Cookies

3 cups	all-purpose flour	750 mL
1 tsp	baking soda	5 mL
$^1/_4$ tsp	salt	1 mL
1 cup	chopped walnuts (optional)	250 mL
1 cup	softened butter	250 mL
$2^1/_2$ cups	firmly packed light brown sugar	625 mL
2	eggs	2
1 tbsp	vanilla	15 mL

VARIATIONS

Almond Icebox Cookies
Substitute 1 cup (250 mL) coarsely chopped slivered almonds for the walnuts.

Cranberry Icebox Cookies
Add $^1/_2$ cup (125 mL) chopped, frozen or fresh cranberries, along with the walnuts.

Preheat oven to 350°F (180°C)
Cookie sheet lined with parchment or waxed paper

1. In a bowl, mix together flour, baking soda, salt and nuts, if using.
2. In another bowl, beat butter and brown sugar until smooth and creamy. Beat in eggs, one at a time, until incorporated. Stir in vanilla. Add flour mixture and mix well.
3. On a lightly floured surface, divide dough in half. Shape into two rolls about 2 inches (5 cm) wide. Wrap each roll tightly in plastic wrap. Refrigerate at least 3 hours or overnight.
4. When ready to bake, remove from wrap and cut dough into slices $^1/_4$ inch (0.5 cm) thick. Place about 2 inches (5 cm) apart on prepared cookie sheet. Bake in preheated oven for 12 to 15 minutes until firm to the touch. Immediately transfer to wire racks to cool completely.

Makes about 6 dozen

Buttery Brown Sugar Slices

$3^1/_2$ cups	all-purpose flour	825 mL
1 tsp	baking soda	5 mL
$^1/_2$ tsp	salt	2 mL
1 cup	softened butter or margarine	250 mL
2 cups	packed brown sugar	500 mL
2	eggs, slightly beaten	2
3 tsp	vanilla	15 mL
1 cup	finely chopped walnuts (optional)	250 mL

HINT: If brown sugar is caked and hard, place it in a jar with half an apple. Close lid tight and let stand for 1 day. Remove apple, fluff up sugar with a fork and put lid on tightly until ready to use.

Preheat oven to 350°F (180°C)
Ungreased cookie sheet

1. In a bowl, combine flour, baking soda and salt.
2. In another bowl, beat butter and brown sugar until smooth and creamy. Beat in eggs, one at a time, until incorporated. Stir in vanilla. Add flour mixture and mix well. Fold in nuts, if using.
3. On a lightly floured surface, divide dough in half. Shape into two rolls about 2 to 3 inches (5 to 7.5 cm) wide. Wrap each tightly in plastic wrap and refrigerate overnight.
4. When ready to bake, remove from wrap and cut dough into slices $^1/_4$ inch (0.5 cm) thick. Place about 2 inches (5 cm) apart on cookie sheet. Bake in preheated oven for 10 to 12 minutes until golden brown. Immediately transfer to wire racks to cool.

Makes about 6 dozen

Butterscotch Pecan Cookies

1¼ cups	all-purpose flour	300 mL
½ tsp	baking powder	2 mL
¼ tsp	salt	1 mL
6 tbsp	softened butter or margarine	90 mL
⅔ cup	packed brown sugar	160 mL
1	egg	1
½ tsp	vanilla	2 mL
½ cup	finely chopped pecans	125 mL

VARIATIONS

Butterscotch Date Cookies
Substitute 2 cups (500 mL) finely chopped dates for the pecans.

Butterscotch Chews
For a soft, chewy cookie, add ¾ cup (175 mL) crushed cornflakes, along with the pecans.

Preheat oven to 350°F (180°C)
Ungreased cookie sheet

1. In a bowl, combine flour, baking powder and salt.

2. In another bowl, beat butter and brown sugar until smooth and creamy. Beat in egg until incorporated. Stir in vanilla. Gradually add flour mixture, mixing until well blended. Fold in pecans.

3. On a lightly floured surface, divide dough in half. Shape into two rolls about 2 inches (5 cm) wide. Wrap each log tightly in plastic wrap and refrigerate at least 2 hours.

4. When ready to bake, remove from wrap and cut dough into slices ¼ inch (0.5 cm) thick. Place about 2 inches (5 cm) apart on cookie sheet. Bake in preheated oven for 10 to 12 minutes until golden brown. Immediately transfer to wire racks to cool.

Makes about 4 dozen

Coffee Break Cinnamon Rolls

1	package (¼ oz/8 g) active dry yeast	1
⅔ cup	warm water	160 mL
2½ cups	biscuit mix	625 mL
¼ cup	packed brown sugar	50 mL
1 tsp	cinnamon	5 mL
½ cup	chopped pecans	125 mL
2 tbsp	melted butter	25 mL
Topping		
¼ cup	melted butter or margarine	50 mL
⅓ cup	packed brown sugar	75 mL
1 tsp	light corn syrup	5 mL

Preheat oven to 400°F (200°C)
Lightly greased jellyroll pan or large cookie sheet

1. In a bowl, dissolve yeast in warm water. Add biscuit mix and beat to form a dough. On a floured surface, knead dough until smooth.

2. In a small bowl, mix together brown sugar, cinnamon and pecans.

3. Roll dough into a 12-inch (30-cm) square and brush with butter. Sprinkle with cinnamon mixture, then roll up like a jellyroll and cut into 12 slices. Place 2 inches (5 cm) apart on pan or sheet and leave in a warm place to rise, about 1 hour. Bake in preheated oven 15 minutes.

4. To make Topping: In a small saucepan, over low heat, melt butter or margarine. Add brown sugar and corn syrup and, stirring constantly, bring to a boil. Five minutes before baking is completed, pour over rolls. Serve warm.

Makes 1 dozen

Mochaccino Cookies

2 cups	all-purpose flour	500 mL
1/4 tsp	salt	1 mL
1 tsp	cinnamon	5 mL
1/2 cup	softened butter or margarine	125 mL
1/2 cup	softened shortening	125 mL
1/2 cup	lightly packed brown sugar	125 mL
1/2 cup	granulated sugar	125 mL
1	egg	1
1 tbsp	instant coffee dissolved in 1 tsp (5 mL) hot water	15 mL
2	squares (each 1 oz/28 g) unsweetened chocolate, melted (see page 11)	2

Chocolate Dip

3 tbsp	shortening	45 mL
1 1/2 cups	semi-sweet chocolate chips	375 mL

HINT: Pack any chilled cookie dough into juice cans. Seal the open end with foil secured by an elastic band. Keep in refrigerator. When ready to use, cut the end out of the can and push the dough out slowly, cutting slices as you push. Place on baking sheets and bake.

Preheat oven to 350°F (180°C)
Lightly greased cookie sheet

1. In a bowl, mix together flour, salt and cinnamon.

2. In another bowl, beat butter or margarine, shortening and sugars until smooth and creamy. Beat in egg. Add coffee mixture and melted chocolate and mix until thoroughly blended. Stir in flour mixture. Cover and refrigerate for at least 1 hour until firm.

3. On lightly floured surface, divide dough in half. Shape into two long logs about 2 to 2 1/2 inches (5 to 6 cm) wide. Wrap each log tightly in plastic wrap and refrigerate at least 2 hours until firm.

4. When ready to bake, remove from wrap and cut dough into slices 1/4 inch (0.5 cm) thick. Place about 2 inches (5 cm) apart on prepared cookie sheet. Bake in preheated oven for 10 to 12 minutes until edges are firm and bottoms are lightly browned. Immediately transfer to wire racks to cool. When cookies are slightly cooled, dip in chocolate, if desired.

5. To make Chocolate Dip: In a saucepan, over low heat, stir shortening and chocolate chips until melted and smooth. Using your fingers, dip top half of each cookie in mixture and place on cookie sheet lined with waxed paper. Refrigerate until chocolate hardens.

Makes about 3 dozen

Fruit and Nut Roly Poly

4 cups	all-purpose flour	1 L
2 tsp	baking powder	10 mL
1/4 tsp	salt	1 mL
4	eggs	4
1 cup	granulated sugar	250 mL
1 cup	vegetable oil	250 mL
1 tsp	vanilla	5 mL
Filling		
1 cup	finely chopped walnuts	250 mL
1/4 cup	granulated sugar	50 mL
1/2 cup	peach preserves	125 mL
1 1/4 cups	diced dried fruits and raisins	300 mL
1 tbsp	grated orange zest	15 mL
1/4 cup	fresh orange juice	50 mL
1/4 cup	melted butter or margarine	50 mL
1/4 cup	fine dry bread crumbs	50 mL

VARIATION

Jam and Nut Roly Poly
On each rolled out portion of dough, spread your favorite jam, leaving a 1/2-inch (1-cm) border. Sprinkle surface with chopped walnuts. Roll and bake, as above. For variety, use different nuts and jam on each portion.

Preheat oven to 375°F (190°C)
Greased cookie sheet

1. In a bowl, sift together flour, baking powder and salt.

2. In another bowl, beat eggs and sugar until light and fluffy. Beat in oil and vanilla until well blended. Stir in dry ingredients until a soft dough forms. (You may not use the entire flour mixture.)

3. To make Filling: In a bowl, mix together walnuts, sugar, peach preserves, dried fruits and raisins, orange zest and juice.

4. On a lightly floured surface, divide dough into four equal portions. Roll one portion into a rectangle about 1/4 inch (0.5 cm) thick. Brush with melted butter or margarine, leaving 1/2-inch (1-cm) border all around. Sprinkle bread crumbs lightly over top and spread one-quarter of the filling over this. Turn ends in and roll dough up like a jellyroll, making sure seam is sealed tight. Repeat with the remaining dough.

5. Place rolls, two at a time, on prepared cookie sheet. Bake in preheated oven for 30 to 35 minutes until nicely browned. Cool on sheets, then cut into 1/2-inch (1-cm) slices.

Makes about 5 dozen

Apricot Cream Cheese Pinwheel Cookies

1	package (8 oz/250 g) softened cream cheese	1
1 cup	softened butter	250 mL
1/4 tsp	salt	1 mL
2 cups	all-purpose flour	500 mL
3/4 cup	apricot preserves	175 mL
1 cup	finely chopped walnuts	250 mL

HINT: Use an electric knife to cut rolled and chilled cookie dough. It makes perfect, even cookies quickly and easily.

Preheat oven to 350°F (180°C)
Lightly greased cookie sheet

1. In a bowl, beat cream cheese, butter and salt until smooth and creamy. Gradually add flour and mix until a soft dough forms. Cover and refrigerate overnight.

2. When ready to bake, combine apricot preserves and nuts in a small bowl.

3. On a lightly floured surface, roll dough into a 12x14 inch (30x35 cm) rectangle. Spread the apricot mixture all over excluding edges. Beginning on one long side, roll up tightly, like a jellyroll. Ensure seam is sealed tight. Cut log in half, horizontally, and wrap each section tightly in plastic wrap. Refrigerate for at least 30 minutes until firm.

4. Remove dough from wrap and cut each log into slices $1/2$ inch (1 cm) thick. Place about 1 inch (2.5 cm) apart on prepared cookie sheet. Bake in preheated oven for 15 minutes until golden. Immediately transfer to wire racks.

Makes about $4^1/2$ to 5 dozen

Cinnamon Roll Slices

3/4 cup	softened butter or margarine	175 mL
1 cup	granulated sugar	250 mL
1 tsp	baking soda	5 mL
3/4 cup	buttermilk (see Hint, page 123)	175 mL
3 cups	all-purpose flour	750 mL
	Softened butter to spread	
	Brown sugar	
	Cinnamon	

Preheat oven to 350°F (180°C)
Lightly greased cookie sheet

1. In a bowl, beat butter or margarine and sugar until smooth and creamy. Mix baking soda with buttermilk and stir into mixture. Gradually stir in flour until a dough forms.

2. On a floured surface, roll dough out to $1/4$-inch (0.5-cm) thickness. Spread with butter, brown sugar and cinnamon. Roll up tightly like a jellyroll, making sure seam is sealed tight, and cut into 1-inch (2.5-cm) slices. Place about 2 inches (5 cm) apart on prepared cookie sheet. Bake in preheated oven for 20 to 25 minutes until lightly browned. Immediately transfer to wire racks to cool.

Makes about 1 dozen

Chocolate 'n' Vanilla Spirals

1¼ cups	all-purpose flour	300 mL
¼ tsp	baking powder	1 mL
¼ tsp	salt	1 mL
½ cup	softened butter or margarine	125 mL
¾ cup	granulated sugar	175 mL
1	egg	1
1 tsp	vanilla	5 mL
1	square (1 oz/28 g) unsweetened chocolate, melted and cooled (see page 11)	1

HINT: For a fun and quick treat, dip the tips of salted pretzel sticks into melted chocolate and then into sprinkles. Place on a plate or a baking sheet covered in waxed paper until chocolate has set.

Preheat oven to 350°F (180°C)
Lightly greased cookie sheet

1. In a bowl, mix together flour, baking powder and salt.

2. In another bowl, beat butter or margarine and sugar until smooth and creamy. Beat in egg until well incorporated. Stir in vanilla. Mix in flour mixture until a soft dough forms.

3. On a lightly floured surface, divide dough in half. Add melted chocolate to one of the halves and knead dough until it is uniformly chocolate colored. Wrap both doughs tightly in plastic wrap and refrigerate for at least 1 hour until dough is firm.

4. When ready to bake, remove from wrap, place plain dough between two sheets of waxed paper and roll out to a 16x6-inch (40x15-cm) rectangle. Remove waxed paper from top of plain dough, but leave waxed paper on bottom. Repeat with chocolate dough. Remove waxed paper from top of chocolate dough and invert chocolate onto the plain dough. Using a rolling pin press together gently. Remove waxed paper from top and trim so both top and bottom are even. Using the waxed paper on the bottom to guide you, and starting from the long edge, roll dough up like a jellyroll, making sure seam is sealed tight. If necessary, roll back and forth on the work surface to make sure the roll is the same diameter from end to end.

5. Wrap tightly in plastic wrap and refrigerate at least 2 hours or overnight. Place roll, seam side down, on a cutting board and cut into slices ¼ inch (0.5 cm) thick. Place 2 inches (5 cm) apart on prepared cookie sheet. Bake in preheated oven for 10 to 12 minutes until lightly browned. Immediately transfer to wire racks to cool.

Makes about 7 dozen

Tri-Color Neapolitan Cookies

Because I have always loved Neapolitan ice cream, these cookies are one of my favorites.

2¹/₂ cups	all-purpose flour	625 mL
¹/₂ tsp	baking powder	2 mL
¹/₂ tsp	salt	2 mL
1 cup	softened butter	250 mL
1¹/₂ cups	granulated sugar	375 mL
1	egg	1
1 tsp	vanilla	5 mL
¹/₂ tsp	almond extract	2 mL
6 drops	red food coloring	6 drops
¹/₂ cup	chopped walnuts	125 mL
¹/₄ cup	cocoa	1 mL

HINT: In place of cocoa, add 1 square (1 oz/28 g) melted unsweetened chocolate to the dough.

Preheat oven to 350°F (180°C)
9x5-inch (1.5-L) loaf pan, bottom and sides lined with waxed paper
Ungreased cookie sheet

1. In a bowl, mix together flour, baking powder and salt.

2. In another bowl, beat butter and sugar until smooth and creamy. Beat in egg until incorporated. Stir in vanilla. Gradually add flour mixture and mix until a soft dough forms.

3. Divide dough into three equal portions. Place one portion in a small bowl. Add almond extract and red food coloring and knead until fully integrated into the dough. Spread this portion evenly over the bottom of the prepared pan. Add nuts to another portion and knead well. Spread this portion evenly over the first layer. Add cocoa to the last portion and knead until it is evenly distributed throughout the dough. Spread this portion over the second layer. Cover with plastic wrap or waxed paper and refrigerate overnight.

4. When ready to bake, remove from pan and cut loaf in half lengthwise. Cut each half into slices ¹/₄ inch (0.5 cm) thick. Place about 2 inches (5 cm) apart on cookie sheet. Bake in preheated oven for 10 to 12 minutes until firm.

Makes about 6 dozen

Apple Fig Date Log

5 cups	all-purpose flour	1.25 L
2 tsp	baking powder	10 mL
1 tsp	baking soda	5 mL
$^1/_2$ tsp	salt	2 mL
1 cup	softened butter	250 mL
1 cup	granulated sugar	250 mL
2	eggs	2
1 cup	sour cream	250 mL
2 tsp	vanilla	10 mL
	Confectioner's (icing) sugar, sifted	

Filling

1$^3/_4$ cups	finely chopped dates	425 mL
1$^3/_4$ cups	finely chopped figs	425 mL
6	peeled, finely chopped Granny Smith apples	6
$^1/_2$ cup	fresh orange juice	125 mL
$^1/_3$ cup	granulated sugar	75 mL
1 cup	chopped walnuts	250 mL

Preheat oven to 350°F (180°C)
Greased cookie sheet

1. In a bowl, combine flour, baking powder, baking soda and salt.

2. In another bowl, beat butter and sugar until smooth and creamy. Beat in eggs, one at a time, until incorporated. Beat in sour cream and vanilla. Gradually add flour mixture, mixing until well blended. Wrap dough tightly in plastic wrap and refrigerate for at least 1 hour.

3. To make Filling: In a large pot, over medium heat, combine dates, figs, apples, orange juice and sugar. Cook, covered, stirring occasionally, for 25 minutes until tender. Remove cover and cook, stirring, until mixture is dry, about 5 minutes. Remove from heat. When cool, mix in walnuts and refrigerate if not using immediately.

4. Divide dough into eight equal portions. On a lightly floured surface, shape one portion into a log, approximately 8 inches (20 cm) long. Roll log into a 10x5-inch (25x12.5-cm) rectangle. Spread $^3/_4$ cup (175 mL) filling down the middle of the rectangle. Fold each side over the filling and pinch together to seal. Place the log, seam side down, on prepared sheet. Repeat with remaining dough and filling.

5. Bake in preheated oven for 25 to 30 minutes until golden brown. Immediately transfer to wire racks to cool. Sift the confectioner's sugar over the logs, then cut into slices $^1/_2$ inches (1 cm) thick.

Makes about 6 dozen

Chocolate Chip Pecan Logs

2 cups	all-purpose flour	500 mL
1/2 tsp	baking powder	2 mL
1/2 tsp	salt	2 mL
1/2 cup	softened butter	125 mL
1	package (4 oz/125 g) softened cream cheese	1
1/2 cup	granulated sugar	125 mL
1/2 cup	lightly packed brown sugar	125 mL
1	egg	1
1 tsp	vanilla	5 mL
Filling		
2/3 cup	semi-sweet chocolate chips	160 mL
2/3 cup	sweetened condensed milk	160 mL
1/2 cup	chopped pecans	125 mL
	Confectioner's (icing) sugar, sifted	

Preheat oven to 350°F (180°C)
Greased cookie sheet

1. In a bowl, mix together flour, baking powder and salt.

2. In another bowl, beat butter, cream cheese and sugars until smooth and creamy. Beat in egg and vanilla. Add flour mixture and mix until a soft dough forms.

3. On a lightly floured surface, divide dough into four portions. Shape each portion into a log, about 8 inches (20 cm) long. Repeat with remaining portions. Refrigerate at least 2 hours.

4. To make Filling: In a small saucepan, over low heat, melt chocolate chips and milk, stirring until smooth. Fold in nuts and set aside.

5. On a well-floured surface, roll each log into a 10x5-inch (25x12.5-cm) rectangle. Spread one-quarter of the filling down the center of the rectangle, leaving about 1 inch (2.5 cm) at the sides so filling won't spill out. Fold into thirds, each side over the filling, to enclose the filling. Trim ends and pinch to seal.

6. Place logs about 2 inches (5 cm) apart, seam side down, on prepared cookie sheet. Bake in preheated oven for 20 to 25 minutes until golden brown. Immediately dust with confectioner's sugar, then transfer to wire racks to cool. Once logs are cool, cut into slices 1/2 inches (1 cm) thick.

Makes about 4 dozen

Glazed Lemon Braids

¹/₂ cup	softened butter or margarine	125 mL
1 cup	granulated sugar	250 mL
1	egg	1
	Zest of 1 lemon	
2 cups	all-purpose flour	500 mL
Glaze		
	Juice of 1 lemon	
1¹/₂ cups	confectioner's (icing) sugar, sifted	375 mL

Preheat oven to 350°F (180°C)
Lightly greased cookie sheet

1. In a bowl, beat butter and sugar until crumbly. Beat in egg and lemon zest. Gradually add flour, mixing thoroughly after each addition until a soft dough forms.

2. Working with ¹/₄ cup (50 mL) of dough at a time, divide in half. Shape each half into 7-inch (17.5-cm) long rope. Entwine the two ropes, as for braiding, then cut in half lengthwise. Place on cookie sheet. Repeat with remaining dough.

3. Chill braids for 30 minutes, then bake in preheated oven until very lightly browned. Immediately transfer to wire racks to cool.

4. To make Glaze: In a bowl, mix together confectioner's sugar and lemon juice. Brush over tops of warm cookies. Let set for 20 minutes.

Makes about 1¹/₂ dozen

Lemon Nutmeg Crisps

1 cup	all-purpose flour	250 mL
¹/₂ tsp	baking powder	2 mL
¹/₂ tsp	baking soda	2 mL
¹/₂ tsp	salt	2 mL
¹/₄ tsp	nutmeg	1 mL
¹/₂ cup	softened butter	125 mL
1¹/₂ cups	confectioner's (icing) sugar, sifted	375 mL
1 tbsp	grated lemon zest	15 mL
2	egg whites	2
¹/₂ tsp	vanilla	2 mL
³/₄ cup	ground walnuts	175 mL

Preheat oven to 300°F (150°C)
Lightly greased cookie sheet

1. In a bowl, mix together flour, baking powder, baking soda, salt and nutmeg.

2. In another bowl, beat butter, confectioner's sugar and lemon zest until smooth. Beat in egg whites. Stir in vanilla and walnuts. Add flour mixture and mix until a soft dough forms. Refrigerate for 2 to 3 hours until firm.

3. On a lightly floured surface, shape into two rolls about 2 inches (5 cm) wide. Wrap tightly in plastic wrap and refrigerate for 2 hours.

4. When ready to bake, remove from wrap and cut into slices ¹/₄ inch (0.5 cm) wide. Place about 2 inches (5 cm) apart on prepared cookie sheet. Bake in preheated oven for 15 to 18 minutes until lightly browned. Immediately transfer to wire racks to cool.

Makes about 5 dozen

Double Almond Sticks

$\frac{1}{2}$ cup	blanched almonds	125 mL
2 tbsp	granulated sugar	25 mL
1 cup	all-purpose flour	250 mL
$\frac{1}{3}$ cup	granulated sugar	75 mL
$\frac{1}{4}$ tsp	salt	1 mL
$\frac{1}{2}$ cup	butter or margarine	125 mL
1	egg yolk	1
$\frac{1}{4}$ tsp	almond extract	1 mL
1	egg white, lightly beaten	1

Preheat oven to 350°F (180°C)
Ungreased cookie sheet
Food processor

1. In a food processor with a metal blade, process almonds until coarsely ground. In a small bowl, mix together 2 tbsp (25 mL) ground almonds with the 2 tbsp (25 mL) sugar and set aside. Set remaining almonds aside.

2. In another bowl, mix together flour, $\frac{1}{3}$ cup (75 mL) sugar, salt and remaining almonds. Using two knives, a pastry blender or your fingers, cut in butter until mixture resembles coarse crumbs. Stir in egg yolk and almond extract, mixing until a soft dough forms.

3. On a lightly floured surface, divide dough into six portions. Flour your hands and roll each portion into a long rope about 12 inches (30 cm) long. Brush tops generously with the beaten egg white and sprinkle with the reserved almond-sugar mixture.

4. Cut each rope into sticks 2 inches (5 cm) long. Place about 1 inch (2.5 cm) apart on cookie sheet. Bake in preheated oven for 15 minutes. Cool for 5 minutes, then transfer to wire racks to cool completely.

Makes about 3 dozen

Raspberry Nut Swirls

1³/₄ cups	all-purpose flour	425 mL
2 tsp	baking powder	10 mL
¼ tsp	salt	1 mL
½ cup	softened butter or margarine	125 mL
1 cup	granulated sugar	250 mL
1	egg	1
1 tsp	vanilla	5 mL
½ cup	raspberry jam	125 mL
⅓ cup	finely chopped walnuts or pecans	75 mL

Preheat oven to 375°F (190°C)
Lightly greased cookie sheet

1. In a bowl, mix together flour, baking powder and salt.

2. In another bowl, beat butter or margarine and sugar until smooth and creamy. Beat in egg until well incorporated. Stir in vanilla. Gradually add flour mixture, mixing until a dough forms. Turn out on a floured work surface and knead lightly.

3. Place dough between two sheets of waxed paper and roll out to a 12x10-inch (30x25-cm) rectangle.

4. In a small bowl, mix together jam and nuts. Spread mixture evenly over the dough, leaving a ½-inch (1-cm) border.

5. Starting at the long edge and using the waxed paper on the bottom as a guide, roll up like a jellyroll, making sure seam is sealed tight. Roll back and forth a couple of times to form an even roll. Wrap tightly in plastic wrap and refrigerate at least overnight.

6. When ready to bake, remove from wrap and cut dough into slices ¼ inch (0.5 cm) thick. Place about 2 inches (5 cm) apart on prepared cookie sheet. Bake in preheated oven for 10 to 15 minutes until golden brown. Immediately transfer to wire racks to cool.

Makes 3½ dozen

Biscotti

Crisp and delicious, biscotti are a traditional Italian biscuit, perfect for dunking in a glass of milk or your morning coffee. Most of my biscotti recipes contain butter, which makes them richer and less crunchy than the traditional Italian versions. But because they are baked twice, they are drier than most other cookies.

Apricot Almond Biscotti

3 cups	all-purpose flour	750 mL
2 tsp	baking powder	10 mL
1/4 tsp	salt	1 mL
3/4 cup	softened butter	175 mL
3/4 cup	granulated sugar	175 mL
2	eggs	2
1 tsp	almond extract	5 mL
1 tsp	orange zest	5 mL
1/2 cup	blanched chopped almonds, toasted (see page 11)	125 mL
1 cup	finely chopped dried apricots	250 mL

HINT: When cutting the partially cooked dough, always use a sharp knife, with a serrated edge and cut in a light sawing motion — otherwise the cookies will crumble.

Preheat oven to 325°F (160°C)
Ungreased cookie sheet

1. In a bowl, mix together flour, baking powder and salt.

2. In another bowl, beat butter and sugar until smooth and creamy. Add eggs, one at a time, beating until well incorporated. Stir in almond extract and orange zest. Add almonds and apricots and mix well. Gradually add flour mixture, mixing until a dough forms.

3. On a lightly floured surface, divide dough in half. Shape into two rolls about 8 inches (20 cm) long. Place at least 2 inches (5 cm) apart on cookie sheet. Bake in preheated oven for 30 to 35 minutes until golden brown.

4. Cool for 5 minutes on cookie sheet, then cut into slices 1/2 inch (1 cm) thick. Place on cookie sheet and return to oven to dry for 15 minutes. Turn slices over and bake for 5 minutes more. Immediately transfer to wire racks to cool.

Makes about 2 1/2 dozen

Chocolate Almond Biscotti

2³/₄ cups	all-purpose flour	675 mL
2¹/₂ tsp	baking powder	12 mL
1 tsp	salt	5 mL
¹/₂ cup	softened butter	125 mL
1¹/₂ cups	granulated sugar	375 mL
2	eggs	2
3	squares (each 1 oz/28 g) semi-sweet chocolate, melted (see page 11)	3
1 tbsp	grated orange zest	15 mL
¹/₄ cup	orange juice	50 mL
3	squares (each 1 oz/28 g) semi-sweet chocolate, coarsely chopped	3
³/₄ cup	walnut pieces, toasted	175 mL
³/₄ cup	whole blanched almonds, toasted	175 mL

NOTE: For an added treat, dip one end of the biscotti in additional melted chocolate.

Preheat oven to 350°F (180°C)
Greased and floured cookie sheet

1. In a bowl, combine flour, baking powder and salt.

2. In another bowl, beat butter and sugar until smooth and creamy. Add eggs, one at a time, beating until incorporated. Stir in melted chocolate. Add orange zest and juice and mix well. Gradually add flour mixture, mixing until a dough forms. Fold in chocolate and nuts.

3. Divide dough in half. Form two rolls about 2 inches (5 cm) wide. Place at least 2 inches (5 cm) apart on prepared sheet. Bake in preheated oven for 30 minutes. Cool on cookie sheet for 10 minutes, then transfer to a cutting board and cut into slices ¹/₂ to ³/₄ inch (1 to 2 cm) thick. Return to oven and bake for 10 minutes. Turn slices over and bake for 10 minutes more. Immediately transfer to wire racks to cool.

Makes about 4 dozen

Chocolate Nut Coffee Biscotti

2 cups	all-purpose flour	500 mL
2 cups	unsweetened cocoa powder	500 mL
2 cups	granulated sugar	500 mL
1 tsp	baking powder	5 mL
1 tsp	baking soda	5 mL
6	eggs	6
Pinch	salt	Pinch
¹/₄ cup	coffee or brandy	50 mL
2 tsp	vanilla	10 mL
2 cups	coarsely chopped walnuts, toasted (see page 11)	500 mL

Preheat oven to 300°F (150°C)
Lightly greased and floured cookie sheet

1. In a bowl, combine flour, cocoa, sugar, baking powder and baking soda. Make a well in center.

2. In another bowl, beat eggs and salt. Add coffee or brandy and vanilla. Pour into well and mix until a soft dough forms. Fold in walnuts.

3. Divide dough in half. Form into two rolls about 10 inches (25 cm) long. Place about 2 inches (5 cm) apart on prepared cookie sheet. Bake in preheated oven for 50 minutes until loaf looks dry. Transfer to a cutting board and cut into slices ¹/₂ inch (1 cm) thick. Return to sheet and bake for 20 minutes. Turn slices over and bake 20 minutes more. Immediately transfer to wire racks.

Makes about 3¹/₂ dozen

Chocolate Chip Biscotti

1³/₄ cups	all-purpose flour	425 mL
2 tsp	baking powder	10 mL
¹/₂ cup	chocolate chips	125 mL
³/₄ cup	whole unblanched almonds	175 mL
2	eggs	2
¹/₃ cup	melted butter	75 mL
³/₄ cup	granulated sugar	175 mL
2 tsp	vanilla	10 mL
1¹/₂ tsp	grated orange zest	7 mL
¹/₂ tsp	almond extract	2 mL
1	egg white, lightly beaten	1

HINT: Chill your rolling pin in the freezer before using so dough will not stick to it.

Preheat oven to 350°F (180°C)
Ungreased cookie sheet

1. In a bowl, combine flour, baking powder, chocolate chips and almonds. Make a well in the center.

2. In another bowl, beat eggs, butter, sugar, vanilla, zest and almond extract. Spoon into well and mix until a sticky dough forms.

3. Divide dough in half, then shape into 2 rolls, 10 to 12 inches (25 to 30 cm) long. Place about 2 inches (5 cm) apart on cookie sheet. Brush tops with egg white. Bake in preheated oven for 20 minutes. Cool on cookie sheet for 5 minutes, then cut into slices ¹/₂ to ³/₄ inch (1 to 2 cm) thick. Stand cookies upright on sheet and bake for another 20 to 25 minutes until golden. Immediately transfer to wire racks to cool.

Makes about 3¹/₂ dozen

Italian-Style Biscotti

3 cups	all-purpose flour	750 mL
2 tsp	baking powder	10 mL
¹/₂ tsp	salt	2 mL
4	eggs, slightly beaten	4
1 cup	granulated sugar	250 mL
¹/₂ cup	melted butter	125 mL
2 tsp	vanilla	10 mL
1 tsp	almond extract	5 mL
2 tsp	anise extract	10 mL
³/₄ cup	finely chopped blanched almonds	175 mL

NOTE: Anise extract is available in many supermarkets. If you can't find it there, try a specialty store.

Preheat oven to 350°F (180°C)
Lightly greased cookie sheet

1. In a bowl, mix together flour, baking powder and salt.

2. In another bowl, beat eggs, sugar and melted butter until well blended. Add extracts and almonds and mix well. Add dry ingredients and mix until a soft dough forms.

3. On a lightly floured surface, divide dough in half. Shape into two rolls, about 12 inches (30 cm) long. Place about 2 inches (5 cm) apart on prepared cookie sheet. Bake in preheated oven for 20 minutes until just beginning to brown around the edges.

4. Cool on sheet for 10 minutes, then transfer to a cutting board and cut into slices ¹/₂ inch (1 cm) thick. Place on sheet and bake for 12 minutes. Turn slices over and bake for 5 to 10 minutes more until golden brown.

Makes about 4 dozen

Cherry Nut Biscotti

2 cups	all-purpose flour	500 mL
1 cup	granulated sugar	250 mL
1 tsp	baking powder	5 mL
2 tsp	lime zest	10 mL
1/4 cup	cold butter, cut into small pieces	50 mL
3/4 cup	dried tart cherries	175 mL
3	eggs	3
1 1/4 cups	shelled pistachios or nuts of your choice	300 mL

Preheat oven to 350°F (180°C)
Greased cookie sheet
Food processor

1. In a food processor, combine flour, sugar, baking powder and zest. Pulse until zest is very fine. Add butter and cherries and pulse until cherries are coarsely chopped.

2. In a bowl, beat eggs lightly. Spoon out 1 tbsp (15 mL) beaten egg and set aside. Add remainder to flour mixture, along with the nuts and pulse until dough is evenly moistened. (The dough will be sticky.)

3. On a well-floured surface, divide dough into four portions. Shape each into rolls 9 inches (22.5 cm) long. Place on prepared sheet at least 2 inches (5 cm) apart. Press lightly to flatten and brush with reserved egg. Bake in preheated oven for 25 minutes until golden brown. Cool on sheets for about 15 minutes, then transfer to a cutting board.

4. Cut into slices 1/2 inch (1 cm) thick and place upright on sheet. Bake 15 minutes more until crisp. Immediately transfer to wire racks to cool.

Makes about 6 dozen

Cinnamon Oatmeal Biscotti

2¹/₂ cups	all-purpose flour	625 mL
1 cup	quick-cooking rolled oats	250 mL
1 tsp	baking powder	5 mL
¹/₄ tsp	baking soda	1 mL
2 tsp	cinnamon	10 mL
¹/₄ tsp	salt	1 mL
1 cup	chopped pecans, toasted (see page 11)	250 mL
¹/₂ cup	softened butter	125 mL
²/₃ cup	packed brown sugar	160 mL
2	eggs	2
¹/₂ cup	liquid honey	125 mL
2 tsp	vanilla	10 mL

HINT: If you run out of brown sugar, make your own by mixing 2 tbsp (25 mL) molasses into 1 cup (250 mL) granulated sugar.

Preheat oven to 350°F (180°C)
Greased cookie sheet

1. In a bowl, mix together flour, oats, baking powder, baking soda, cinnamon, salt and pecans.

2. In another bowl, beat butter and brown sugar until smooth and creamy. Beat in eggs, one at a time, until well incorporated. Mix in honey, then vanilla. Add flour mixture and mix until well combined.

3. Divide dough in half. Shape into two rolls about 10 inches (25 cm) long. Place about 2 inches (5 cm) apart on prepared cookie sheet. Bake in preheated oven for 30 minutes until lightly brown. Cool on sheet for 5 minutes, then transfer to a cutting board and cut into slices ¹/₂ inch (1 cm) thick. Stand slices up on sheet and reduce oven heat to 325°F (160°C). Bake for 25 to 30 minutes longer until golden brown. Immediately transfer to wire racks to cool.

Makes about 3 dozen

Coffee House Biscotti

2 cups + 2 tbsp	all-purpose flour	500 mL + 25 mL
1 tsp	baking powder	5 mL
1/4 tsp	salt	1 mL
1/2 cup	softened butter	125 mL
1 cup	granulated sugar	250 mL
2	eggs	2
1 tsp	vanilla	5 mL
	Grated zest of 1 large lemon	
1 cup	coarsely chopped hazelnuts, toasted (see page 11)	250 mL

Preheat oven to 350°F (180°C)
Ungreased cookie sheet

1. In a bowl, combine flour, baking powder and salt.
2. In another bowl, beat butter and sugar until smooth and creamy. Beat in eggs, one at a time, until incorporated. Mix in vanilla and lemon zest. Gradually add flour mixture, mixing until a soft dough forms. Fold in nuts.
3. Divide dough in half. Shape into two rolls about 10 inches (25 cm) long. Place about 2 inches (5 cm) apart on cookie sheet. Bake in preheated oven for 30 minutes until golden. Cool on sheet for 10 minutes, then transfer to a cutting board and cut into slices 1/2 inch (1 cm) thick. Return to sheet and bake for 10 minutes until lightly browned. Turn slices over and bake 10 minutes more. Immediately transfer to wire racks.

Makes about 3 dozen

Cranberry Pistachio Biscotti

3 cups	all-purpose flour	750 mL
3 tsp	baking powder	15 mL
1/4 tsp	salt	1 mL
3	eggs	3
3/4 cup	granulated sugar	175 mL
1/2 cup	melted butter	125 mL
2 tsp	vanilla	10 mL
1/3 cup	chopped dried cranberries	75 mL
1/2 cup	unsalted pistachios or almonds	125 mL

Preheat oven to 350°F (180°C)
Greased cookie sheet

1. In a bowl, combine flour, baking powder and salt.
2. In another bowl, beat eggs, sugar, butter and vanilla until blended. Gradually add dry ingredients until a sticky dough forms. Using floured hands, work in cranberries and nuts until evenly distributed and dough is smooth.
3. Divide dough in half. Shape into two rolls about 10 inches (25 cm) long. Place about 2 inches (5 cm) apart on prepared cookie sheet. Bake in preheated oven for 20 minutes until browned. Cool on sheet for 10 minutes, then cut into slices 1/2 to 3/4 inch (1 to 2 cm) thick. Arrange slices upright on cookie sheet. Lower oven heat to 300°F (150°C) and bake for 20 to 25 minutes until firm and dry. Immediately transfer to wire racks.

Makes about 3 dozen

Lemon–Orange Cocoa Biscotti

3 cups	all-purpose flour	750 mL
1 cup	granulated sugar	250 mL
5$\frac{1}{2}$ tsp	baking powder	27 mL
$\frac{1}{2}$ tsp	salt	2 mL
$\frac{3}{4}$ cup	unsweetened cocoa	175 mL
$\frac{1}{2}$ cup	coarsely chopped slivered almonds, toasted (see page 11)	125 mL
$\frac{1}{2}$ cup	melted butter	125 mL
$\frac{1}{2}$ cup	water	125 mL
4	eggs	4
1 tsp	vanilla	5 mL
	Grated zest of 3 lemons	
	Grated zest of 2 oranges	

Preheat oven to 375°F (190°C)
Lightly greased cookie sheet

1. In a bowl, combine flour, sugar, baking powder, salt, cocoa and almonds. Make a well in the center.

2. In another bowl, whisk butter, water, eggs, vanilla, lemon and orange zests. Pour into well and mix until a stiff dough forms.

3. Divide dough in half. Shape into two rolls about 12x3 inches (30x7.5 cm). Place about 2 inches (5 cm) apart on prepared cookie sheet. Bake in preheated oven for 25 to 30 minutes. Immediately cut into slices $\frac{1}{2}$ to $\frac{3}{4}$ inch (1 to 2 cm) thick.

4. Lower oven heat to 350°F (180°C). Place slices on cookie sheet and bake for 10 minutes. Turn slices over and bake for 10 minutes more. Immediately transfer to wire racks.

Makes about 4 dozen

Lemon Almond Biscotti

1$\frac{3}{4}$ cups	all-purpose flour	425 mL
$\frac{3}{4}$ cup	granulated sugar	175 mL
1 tbsp	baking powder	15 mL
2 tbsp	finely grated lemon zest	25 mL
$\frac{3}{4}$ cup	coarsely chopped almonds	175 mL
2	eggs	2
$\frac{1}{3}$ cup	olive oil	75 mL
1 tsp	vanilla	5 mL
$\frac{1}{2}$ tsp	almond extract	2 mL

Preheat oven to 325°F (160°C)
Greased cookie sheet

1. In a bowl, mix together flour, sugar, baking powder, lemon zest and almonds. Make a well in the center.

2. In another bowl, whisk eggs, oil, vanilla and almond extract. Pour into well and mix until a soft, sticky dough forms.

3. Divide dough in half. Shape into two rolls about 10 inches (25 cm) long. Place about 2 inches (5 cm) apart on prepared cookie sheet. Bake in preheated oven for 20 minutes.

4. Cool on sheet for 5 minutes, then cut into slices $\frac{1}{2}$ inch (1 cm) thick. Return to sheet and bake for 10 minutes. Turn slices over and bake for 10 minutes more. Immediately transfer to wire racks.

Makes about 3 dozen

Specialty Cookies

In this section of the book I've collected recipes for cookies that are a bit unusual. They may be special because they are put to extraordinary uses, such as being shaped into cups or cones and packed with a filling or, like Best Spritz Cookies, they are pressed into interesting patterns and designs using an uncommon technique. Try browsing through this chapter when you're in the mood to make cookies but feel you want something different.

Apricot Cheddar Pillows

2 cups	all-purpose flour	500 mL
1/2 tsp	salt	2 mL
1/3 cup	butter	75 mL
2/3 cup	shortening	160 mL
1/2 lb	old Cheddar cheese, crumbled, about 1 cup (250 mL)	250 g
1 to 2 tbsp	cold water (optional)	15 to 25 mL
1/2 cup	apricot jam	125 mL

Preheat oven to 400°F (200°C)
Ungreased cookie sheet
Round cookie cutter

1. In a bowl, mix together flour and salt. Using two knives, a pastry blender or your fingers, cut in butter and shortening until mixture resembles coarse crumbs. Mix in crumbled cheese. If necessary, add enough cold water to dough to achieve a pastry-like consistency. Knead lightly and refrigerate for at least 30 minutes.

2. On a lightly floured surface, roll dough out to 1/8-inch (0.25-cm) thickness. Using a round cookie cutter or glass dipped in flour, cut out circles. Place a level teaspoonful (5 mL) apricot jam in the center of each round. Fold dough in half to form a semi-circle. Seal edges with the tines of a fork. Place about 1/2 inch (1 cm) apart on cookie sheet. Bake in preheated oven for 12 to 15 minutes until golden brown. Immediately transfer to wire racks to cool.

Makes about 3 dozen

Chocolate Puffs

1	package (8 oz/235 g) refrigerated crescent rolls	1
1	milk chocolate or bittersweet chocolate bar (4 oz/100 g), broken into four equal pieces	1

Preheat oven to 375°F (190°C)
Ungreased cookie sheet

1. On a floured surface, separate dough into four rectangles and press the perforated seams together to form a seamless piece.

2. Place a piece of chocolate in the center of each rectangle. Fold up the sides of dough to cover the chocolate, making certain the chocolate is totally enclosed and won't leak out. Pinch the seams together to form a new rectangle about 4 1/2 x 2 1/2 inches (11x6 cm). Repeat with remaining dough. Place about 2 inches (5 cm) apart on cookie sheet. Bake in preheated oven for 10 to 12 minutes until golden brown. Cool on sheet for a few minutes, then transfer to a serving plate.

Makes 4 puffs

Cookie Cups

¹/₂ cup	all-purpose flour	125 mL
¹/₂ cup	granulated sugar	125 mL
Pinch	salt	Pinch
1	egg	1
1	egg white	1
1 tsp	orange liqueur	5 mL
1 tsp	grated orange zest	5 mL
3 tbsp	butter or margarine, melted	45 mL
¹/₄ cup	sliced blanched almonds, toasted (see page 11)	50 mL
	Pudding, mousse or fresh fruit for filling	
	Whipped cream	

Preheat oven to 350°F (180°C)
Greased cookie sheet
Small custard cups inverted or overturned muffin tin, brushed with butter

1. In a bowl, combine flour, sugar and salt.

2. In another bowl, whisk together egg, egg white, liqueur and zest. Gradually stir in flour mixture and mix until blended and smooth. Fold in toasted almonds.

3. Drop batter by heaping tablespoons (15 mL), 4 inches (10 cm) apart and 4 inches (10 cm) from the edge, onto prepared cookie sheet. Bake only two cookies at a time in preheated oven for 5 to 7 minutes until edges are lightly browned.

4. Working quickly with a spatula, drape warm cookies, one at a time, over the inverted cups and press down lightly with your hand to make a cup shape. When cookies become firm, about 30 minutes, lift gently and place on a rack to cool.

5. To serve: Fill cookie cups with pudding, mousse or fresh fruit topped with whipped cream.

Makes 1 dozen cookie cups

Cinnamon Pretzels

³/₄ cup	warm water	175 mL
1	package (16 oz/500 g) hot roll mix with yeast or frozen pizza dough, thawed	1
¹/₃ cup	granulated sugar	75 mL
3	egg yolks, divided	3
¹/₄ cup	orange juice	50 mL
1 tsp	grated orange zest (optional)	5 mL
2 tbsp	melted butter	25 mL
1 tsp	cinnamon	5 mL
1 tsp	vanilla	5 mL
Topping		
2 tbsp	granulated sugar	25 mL
¹/₂ tsp	cinnamon	2 mL

Preheat oven to 350°F (180°C)
Greased cookie sheet

1. In a large bowl, combine the hot roll mix or frozen pizza dough with yeast package, water, sugar, 2 egg yolks, juice, zest, if using, butter, cinnamon and vanilla. Mix together until well blended and a soft dough forms.

2. On a lightly floured surface, knead dough for 5 minutes until smooth and elastic. Cover and let rest for 5 minutes.

3. Divide dough into 16 portions. Roll each portion out into a 6-inch (15-cm) long rope. Place one portion on prepared sheet.

4. Shape into a heart shape. Twist dough ends twice where they meet and attach ends to the curved bottom of the heart to form a pretzel shape. Repeat with remaining dough.

5. In a small bowl, whisk remaining egg yolk with 1 tbsp (15 mL) water. Brush over top of pretzels.

6. To make Topping: In another bowl, mix together sugar and cinnamon. Sprinkle over pretzels. Let rise for 10 minutes.

7. Bake in preheated oven for 20 minutes or until golden brown. Immediately transfer to racks to cool.

Makes 16 pretzels

Swedish Rosettes

1 cup	all-purpose flour	250 mL
2 tbsp	granulated sugar	25 mL
Pinch	salt	Pinch
2	eggs	2
1 cup	milk	250 mL
	Oil for frying	
3/4 cup	confectioner's (icing) sugar, sifted	175 mL

NOTE: Rosette irons can be purchased at kitchen accessory stores.

Rosette iron
Deep fryer or Dutch oven

1. In a bowl, mix together flour, sugar and salt. Make a well in the center.

2. In a bowl, whisk eggs and milk until blended. Gradually spoon into well, stirring until blended and smooth. Cover and chill in refrigerator for 1 hour.

3. In a deep fryer or Dutch oven, heat oil to 375°F (190°C). Dip rosette iron into hot oil for about 1 minute. Tap off excess oil and dip iron into batter until about three-quarters of it is submerged in the batter. However, do not allow batter to cover the top of the iron. If the batter won't stick the iron is probably too hot, so allow it to cool slightly.

4. Return iron to oil and fry until the rosette slips off the iron. Continue cooking the rosette for 35 to 40 seconds until golden. If rosette does not come off iron, loosen sides gently with a knife. With a slotted spoon, transfer the rosette from the oil to paper towels to drain. Repeat, stirring the batter each time before dipping, until all batter is used up. When cooled, sprinkle rosettes with confectioner's sugar.

Makes about 6 dozen

Almond Cookie Cones

2 tbsp	corn syrup	25 mL
4 tsp	maple syrup	20 mL
2 tbsp	softened butter	25 mL
4 tsp	liquid honey	20 mL
½ cup	granulated sugar	125 mL
3 tbsp	whipping cream	45 mL
1 tsp	all-purpose flour	5 mL
¾ cup	ground almonds	175 mL

White Chocolate Cream Filling

3	squares (each 1 oz/28 g) 3 chopped white chocolate	
¾ cup	heavy cream, divided	175 mL

HINT: Leftover whipped cream will retain its lightness and texture for a day or more, refrigerated, if you add 1 tsp (5 mL) light corn syrup to each ½ pint cream. You won't notice any more sweetness with this addition.

NOTE: Fill the cones with plain whipped cream or whipped cream mixed with chopped strawberries.

Preheat oven to 400°F (200°C)

Lightly oiled cookie sheet lined with parchment or waxed paper

1. In a medium saucepan, combine syrups, butter, honey, sugar, cream and flour. Bring to a boil and, over medium heat, cook, stirring, for about 5 minutes. Remove from heat and stir in almonds.

2. Using a ladle or large spoon, drop one-sixth of the batter onto prepared cookie sheet to form a round cookie. Repeat two more times, so there are three cookies on the sheet, leaving enough room between each cookie to allow for considerable spreading.

3. Bake in preheated oven for 5 to 6 minutes until cookies are golden. Cool on sheet for 3 minutes, then carefully loosen the edges with a spatula or knife. Lift cookie and wrap it around well-greased handles of several spoons held together to form a cone. Cool, then slide off gently. Or place lacy side of a cooled cookie on a foil-lined baking sheet and heat in a 350°F (180°C) oven for 2 to 3 minutes until it softens slightly. Remove from foil, one cookie at a time, and roll, lacy side out, to form cones. Repeat with remaining batter.

4. To make White Chocolate Cream Filling: In a small saucepan, over low heat, melt chocolate and ¼ cup (50 mL) cream, stirring until smooth. Set aside to cool. In a bowl, beat remaining ½ cup (125 mL) cream until soft peaks form. Fold in chocolate mixture and refrigerate until ready to use. When ready to serve, spoon about 2 tbsp (25 mL) mixture into each cornucopia.

Makes 6 cones

Almond Crescents

2 cups	cake flour	500 mL
1/2 cup	confectioner's (icing) sugar, sifted	125 mL
1 cup	softened butter	250 mL
1 tsp	vanilla	5 mL
1 cup	finely chopped almonds	250 mL
	Confectioner's (icing) sugar, sifted	

Preheat oven to 350°F (180°C)
Cookie sheet lined with parchment or waxed paper

1. In a bowl, sift flour and confectioner's sugar.

2. In another bowl, cream butter until smooth. Add vanilla and mix well. Stir in flour mixture until well blended. Fold in almonds. Refrigerate dough for at least 4 hours until firm.

3. On a lightly floured surface, shape 1 tbsp (15 mL) dough into a roll 2 to 2 1/2 inches (5 to 6 cm) long. Bend ends inward to form a crescent shape. Repeat with remaining dough. Place about 2 inches (5 cm) apart on prepared cookie sheet. Bake in preheated oven for 12 to 15 minutes until firm to the touch and golden brown. Transfer to wire racks to cool, then sprinkle with confectioner's sugar.

Makes about 4 dozen

Sugar-Coated Walnut Crescents

1 1/2 cups	softened butter	375 mL
2 tbsp	confectioner's (icing) sugar, sifted	25 mL
1	egg yolk, beaten	1
1 cup	finely chopped walnuts	250 mL
3 1/4 cups	all-purpose flour	800 mL
	Additional confectioner's (icing) sugar, sifted, for coating	

Preheat oven to 300°F (150°C)
Cookie sheet lined with parchment or waxed paper

1. In a bowl, cream butter and confectioner's sugar until smooth. Add beaten egg yolk and chopped walnuts. Mix together until well blended. Gradually add flour and mix until a soft dough forms. Cover and refrigerate for 1 hour until firm.

2. On a lightly floured surface, form dough into 1 1/4-inch (3-cm) balls. Shape each into a log about 3 inches (7.5 cm) long with tapering ends. Bend each end inward to form a crescent. Place about 2 inches (5 cm) apart on cookie sheet. Bake in preheated oven for 35 to 40 minutes until lightly browned on the bottom and almost firm to the touch. Cool slightly on sheet.

4. Sift confectioner's sugar onto a clean cookie sheet until it forms a thin layer. Arrange crescents on sugar and sift additional confectioner's sugar over tops. Let stand until cool.

Makes about 3 dozen

Cheddar–Chive Tomato Pinwheels

4 1/2 cups	all-purpose flour	1.125 L
1	package (1/4 oz/8 g) active dry yeast	1
2 tbsp	granulated sugar	25 mL
1 1/4 tsp	salt	6 mL
1/4 cup	softened butter or margarine	50 mL
1/2 cup	warm water (not hot)	125 mL
3/4 cup	warmed tomato juice	175 mL
1	egg	1
2 tbsp	finely chopped chives	25 mL
2 cups	finely shredded Cheddar cheese	500 mL

Preheat oven to 400°F (200°C)
Greased bowl
Greased cookie sheet

1. In a bowl, mix together flour, yeast, sugar and salt.

2. Add butter or margarine, water, tomato juice and egg and beat well. Gradually add flour mixture until a soft dough forms. (You may not use all the flour.) Shape dough into a ball and place in bowl, turning to ensure that all sides of the dough are greased. Cover and refrigerate for 2 to 3 hours until dough has doubled in size. Using your fists, as in making bread, punch dough down. Divide into two portions.

3. On a floured surface, roll one portion of dough into a 15x12-inch (37.5x30-cm) rectangle, about 1/8 inch (0.25 cm) thick. Using a pastry wheel or a sharp knife cut into 3-inch (7.5-cm) squares. Place about 1 inch (2.5 cm) apart on prepared cookie sheet. Cut 1-inch (2.5-cm) slits from each corner to the center.

4. In a small bowl, mix together chives and cheese.

5. Place 1 rounded teaspoonful (5 mL) chive mixture in the center of each square. Bring alternate corners up to the center, overlapping slightly, to form a pinwheel. Press firmly in the center to seal. Repeat with remaining dough. Bake in preheated oven for 8 to 10 minutes until golden brown. Immediately transfer to wire racks to cool.

Makes about 40 pinwheels

Cookie Cards

These cookies are a unique and fun way to make place cards.

2¹⁄₄ cups	all-purpose flour	550 mL
1¹⁄₂ tsp	baking powder	7 mL
¹⁄₄ tsp	salt	1 mL
³⁄₄ cup	softened shortening	175 mL
1 cup	granulated sugar	250 mL
2	eggs	2
1 tsp	vanilla	5 mL
	Icings	
	Cake decorator for printing names	
	Strands of red shoestring licorice, colored ribbon, wool or string	

Preheat oven to 375°F (190°C)
Rectangular cookie cutter, preferably with fluted edges
Ungreased cookie sheet
Drinking straw
Cookie cutter

1. In a bowl, mix together flour, baking powder and salt.

2. In another bowl, beat shortening and sugar until smooth and creamy. Add eggs, one at a time, beating until well incorporated. Stir in vanilla. Gradually add flour mixture and mix until a dough forms.

3. On a lightly floured surface, roll dough out to ¹⁄₈-inch (0.25-cm) thickness. Using a cookie cutter dipped in flour, cut out shapes and place 2 inches (5 cm) apart on sheet. Using a drinking straw, punch two holes into the dough on one long side of the rectangle. Bake in preheated oven for 6 to 8 minutes until lightly browned. Immediately transfer to wire racks to cool.

4. Decorate and print names on with icing.

5. To make place cards: Place two cookies together and thread a ribbon or licorice through the holes. Make a bow or a knot in the back and stand cards up.

Makes about 18 name cards, depending on the size of cookie cutter used

Homemade Ladyfingers

2	egg yolks	2
1/2 tsp	vanilla	2 mL
Pinch	salt	Pinch
3	egg whites, room temperature	3
1/3 cup + 3 tbsp	granulated sugar	75 mL + 45 mL
1/3 cup	all-purpose flour	75 mL

NOTE: Ladyfinger tins are molds that ladyfingers are baked in. If you have them, just spoon the mixture into each mold and bake as above.

Preheat oven to 350°F (180°C)
Greased cookie sheet
Pastry bag

1. In a bowl, whisk together egg yolks, vanilla and salt until thick and pale yellow in color.

2. In another bowl, beat egg whites until soft peaks form. Gradually add 1/3 cup (75 mL) sugar, beating until stiff peaks form. Fold into egg yolk mixture, then gradually fold in flour until well combined.

3. Fill a pastry bag with batter. Pipe fingers, about 4 to 5 inches (10 to 12.5 cm) long, 2 inches (5 cm) apart onto prepared cookie sheet. Sprinkle lightly with remaining sugar. Bake in preheated oven for 10 to 12 minutes until lightly browned. Immediately transfer to wire racks to cool.

Makes about 20 ladyfingers

Special Wonton Cookies

Wonton wrappers, or squares of dough, can be purchased at most major grocery stores.

1 1/2 cups	packed brown sugar	375 mL
1 cup	chopped dried apricots	250 mL
1 1/2 cups	chopped prunes	375 mL
1 cup	chopped almonds	250 mL
1 1/2 cups	flaked or shredded coconut	375 mL
24	wonton squares	24
	Vegetable oil for frying	

Deep fryer or Dutch oven

1. In a bowl, mix together sugar, apricots, prunes, almonds and coconut.

2. Lay half the wonton squares out on a work surface. Place about 2 tsp (10 mL) filling in the center of each. Moisten edges with water and fold in half to form a triangle. Press edges together firmly to seal. Repeat until all wrappers are filled. Cover filled wontons with a cloth to keep moist.

3. Fill a deep fryer or Dutch oven with oil to a depth of about 1 1/2 inches (4 cm). Heat to 360°F (180°C). Using a slotted spoon, drop four wontons at a time into the hot oil, and cook, turning, until golden brown. Lift out with the slotted spoon and drain on paper towel.

Makes 2 dozen

Fortune Cookies

Before beginning these cookies, make up about 24 paper fortunes, about 2x½ inches (5x1 cm), with clever little sayings, to place inside.

½ cup	all-purpose flour	125 mL
1 tbsp	cornstarch	15 mL
¼ cup	granulated sugar	50 mL
Pinch	salt	Pinch
¼ cup	cooking oil	50 mL
2	egg whites	2
1 tsp	almond extract	5 mL

HINT: If a cookie cools before you can form it, heat in 300°F (150°C) preheated oven for about 1 minute.

Preheat oven to 300°F (150°C)
Greased cookie sheet
Waxed paper
Ungreased muffin tin

1. In a bowl, mix together flour, cornstarch, sugar and salt. Make a well in the center.

2. In another bowl, whisk oil, egg whites and almond extract. Pour into well and stir until mixture is blended and smooth.

3. Spoon a heaping teaspoonful (5 mL) batter onto prepared cookie sheet. Using the back of a spoon, spread into a 3-inch (7.5-cm) circle. Make three other circles. (Cookies will spread, so bake only four at a time.) Bake in preheated oven for 10 minutes until golden brown.

4. Working quickly, one cookie at a time, and using a wide spatula, flip cookies from baking sheet onto a sheet of waxed paper. Place a paper fortune in the center and fold cookie in half. Gently bring tips of cookie together to form a slight crease or bend in the middle. Place cookie in an ungreased muffin cup to cool and to hold its shape. Repeat with remaining dough.

Makes about 2 dozen

Sugar Cinnamon Twists

³/₄ cup	warm water, divided	175 mL
1	package (¹/₄ oz/8 g) active dry yeast	1
¹/₄ cup	softened butter or margarine	50 mL
¹/₄ cup	granulated sugar	50 mL
1	egg	1
4 to 4¹/₂ cups	all-purpose flour, divided	1 to 1.125 L
1¹/₂ tsp	salt	7 mL
¹/₂ cup	warm milk	125 mL
Filling		
¹/₂ cup	packed brown sugar	125 mL
4 tsp	cinnamon	20 mL
¹/₄ cup	melted butter or margarine	50 mL

HINT: If your recipe calls for eggs at room temperature and you forgot to remove them from the refrigerator, place them in warm water for several minutes.

Preheat oven to 350°F (180°C)
Greased bowl
Greased cookie sheet

1. In a bowl, combine yeast and ¹/₄ cup/50 mL water. Stir until dissolved.

2. Add butter or margarine, sugar, egg, 2 cups (500 mL) flour, salt, remaining water and milk. Beat for 2 to 3 minutes until blended. Gradually add more flour, mixing until a soft dough forms.

3. On a floured surface, knead dough for 6 to 8 minutes until smooth and elastic. Place dough in bowl, turning to ensure that all sides of the dough are greased. Cover and let rise in a warm place for about 1 hour until dough doubles in size. Punch down, then roll out to a 16x12-inch (40x30-cm) rectangle.

4. To make Filling: In a small bowl, mix together brown sugar and cinnamon. Brush dough with melted butter or margarine, then sprinkle with sugar-cinnamon mixture.

5. Let dough rest for 5 minutes, then cut lengthwise into three strips, 16x4 inches (40x10 cm). Cut each strip into 16 pieces, 4x1 inches (10x2.5 cm). Twist each strip and place on prepared sheets. Cover with a cloth and let rise for about 30 minutes until doubled in size.

6. Bake in preheated oven for 5 minutes until golden brown. Immediately transfer to wire racks to cool.

Makes 4 dozen twists

Oatmeal Pecan Turnovers

2¹/₂ cups	all-purpose flour	625 mL
1 tsp	baking powder	5 mL
¹/₂ tsp	baking soda	2 mL
1 tsp	salt	5 mL
2 cups	old-fashioned rolled oats	500 mL
¹/₂ cup	chopped pecans	125 mL
¹/₂ cup	softened butter or margarine	125 mL
1 cup	packed brown sugar	250 mL
1	egg	1
1 tsp	vanilla	5 mL
¹/₂ cup	milk	125 mL
1	package (8 oz/250 g) softened cream cheese	1
1 cup	fruit pie filling	250 mL
	Confectioner's (icing) sugar, sifted	

Preheat oven to 375°F (190°C)
Greased cookie sheet

1. In a bowl, mix together flour, baking powder, baking soda, salt, oats and pecans.

2. In another bowl, beat butter or margarine and brown sugar until smooth and creamy. Beat in egg until incorporated. Stir in vanilla and milk. Mix in dry ingredients until well blended and a soft dough forms. Cover and refrigerate for 30 minutes.

3. Place dough between two sheets of waxed paper and roll out to ¹/₄-inch (0.5-cm) thickness. Remove paper and cut into 4-inch (10-cm) squares. Spoon 1 tbsp (15 mL) cream cheese onto half of each square. Top with 1 tbsp (15 mL) fruit pie filling. Fold into a triangle and press edges with the tines of a fork dipped in flour to seal. Place about 2 inches (5 cm) apart on prepared cookie sheet. Bake in preheated oven for 20 to 25 minutes until crispy and golden brown. Transfer to wire racks to cool. Sprinkle with confectioner's sugar.

Makes 16 turnovers

Fancy Lattice Cookies

$2/3$ cup	all-purpose flour	160 mL
$1/4$ tsp	cinnamon	1 mL
$1/4$ tsp	cloves	1 mL
$1/4$ tsp	nutmeg	1 mL
1	package (18 oz/540 g) refrigerated sugar cookie dough	1
	Seedless raspberry jam	
	Confectioner's (icing) sugar, sifted	

Preheat oven to 350°F (180°C)
Ungreased cookie sheet
Cookie cutter

1. In a bowl, mix together flour, cinnamon, cloves and nutmeg. Add sugar cookie dough and knead together until well combined.

2. Place dough between two sheets of waxed paper and roll out to $1/8$-inch (0.25-cm) thickness. Remove top sheet and using a cookie cutter or a glass dipped in flour, cut out 2-inch (5-cm) rounds. Shape remaining scraps of dough into a disk and set aside.

3. Place rounds about 1 inch (2.5 cm) apart on cookie sheet. Spread each with $1/2$ tsp (2 mL) jam.

4. Place disk of scrap dough between two sheets of waxed paper and roll out to $1/8$-inch (0.25-cm) thickness. Cut dough into 2x$1/4$-inch (5x0.5-cm) strips. Place strips over the jam on each cookie to form a lattice pattern, two strips horizontally and two strips intertwined vertically. Trim to fit.

5. Bake in preheated oven for 15 minutes until golden brown. Cool on sheet for 2 minutes, then transfer to wire racks to cool completely. Sprinkle with confectioner's sugar.

Makes about 2$1/2$ dozen

Peak Frean Vanilla Napoleons

1	package (4-serving size) vanilla pudding and pie filling mix	1
1 1/2 cups	milk	375 mL
1/2 cup	confectioner's (icing) sugar, sifted	125 mL
1 tbsp	water	15 mL
1/4 tsp	vanilla	1 mL
24	Peak Frean Nice cookies	24
1	square (1 oz/28 g) unsweetened chocolate, melted (see page 11)	1

1. Prepare pudding following package directions, but using only 1 1/2 cups (375 mL) milk. Allow to cool, stirring frequently.

2. In a bowl, mix together sugar, water and vanilla to make a glaze.

3. Place eight cookies on a work surface. Spread tops with the glaze. Using a spoon, drizzle with chocolate in thin horizontal lines about 1/2 inch (1 cm) apart. Draw a knife across the lines in the opposite direction (vertically) to make a design. Set aside.

4. Place eight more cookies on work surface. Spread each with pudding. Top with eight more cookies and spread with pudding. Top with glazed cookies. Refrigerate for 6 hours.

Makes 8 napoleons

Delicate Lace Baskets

1/4 cup	butter	50 mL
1/4 cup	granulated sugar	50 mL
2 1/2 tbsp	dark molasses	32 mL
1/4 tsp	cinnamon	1 mL
Pinch	ground ginger	Pinch
1 1/2 tsp	vanilla	7 mL
1/3 cup	all-purpose flour	75 mL
	Pudding, mousse or ice cream for filling	

Preheat oven to 300°F (150°C)
Greased cookie sheet
4-inch (10-cm) diameter bowl, brushed with melted butter

1. In a saucepan, over medium heat, melt butter with sugar, molasses, cinnamon and ginger, stirring until mixture is smooth. Stir in vanilla, then flour, until blended.

2. Using a large spoon, drop 2 1/2 tbsp (32 mL) batter, about 4 inches (10 cm) apart, onto prepared cookie sheet. (Cookies will spread, so bake only three at a time.) Bake in preheated oven for 18 minutes. Cool on sheet for 30 seconds, then using a wide spatula, lift cookies up and carefully shape over the bottom of prepared bowl. Allow to cool on bowl until cookie is firm, then gently lift off. Repeat with remaining batter.

3. Fill cooled baskets with pudding, mousse or ice cream.

Makes 6 baskets

Best Spritz Cookies

"Spritz" are cookies put through a cookie press. They are great fun because you can make so many interesting patterns and designs.

1 cup	softened butter	250 mL
1 cup	granulated sugar	250 mL
1	egg	1
1/4 tsp	salt	1 mL
2 tsp	vanilla	10 mL
2 1/4 cups	all-purpose flour	550 mL

VARIATIONS

Lemon Spritz
Omit egg and vanilla and add 1/4 cup (50 mL) frozen lemonade concentrate.

Cinnamon Spritz
Substitute 1 1/3 cups (325 mL) lightly packed brown sugar for the granulated sugar. Add 1 tsp (5 mL) cinnamon.

Chocolate Spritz
Add 2 squares (each 1 oz/28 g) melted unsweetened chocolate.

Preheat oven to 400°F (200°C)
Cookie press
Ungreased cookie sheet

1. In a bowl, beat butter and sugar until smooth and creamy. Add egg and beat until well incorporated. Stir in salt and vanilla. Add flour and beat until blended. If dough is too soft, cover and chill in refrigerator for about 30 minutes until firm.

2. Pack dough into cookie press and press cookies onto baking sheet about 1 inch (2.5 cm) apart. Bake in preheated oven for 6 to 8 minutes until edges are lightly browned. Cool on sheet for 5 minutes, then transfer to wire racks to cool completely.

Makes about 7 dozen

Sandwich Cookies

The appeal of sandwich cookies is obvious. What could be better than a freshly baked cookie? Two freshly baked cookies spread with a mouth-watering filling and pressed together. I hope you'll try some of these delicious treats.

Chocolate Cream Delights

2¹/₂ cups	all-purpose flour	625 mL
1 tsp	baking powder	5 mL
1 tsp	salt	5 mL
³/₄ cup	softened shortening	175 mL
1 cup	granulated sugar	250 mL
2	eggs	2
¹/₂ tsp	vanilla	2 mL
3	squares (each 1 oz/28 g) unsweetened chocolate, melted (see page 11)	3
	Sugar	

Filling

¹/₂ cup	softened butter	125 mL
1¹/₂ cups	confectioner's (icing) sugar, sifted	375 mL
2	egg yolks	2
2 tsp	vanilla	10 mL

VARIATION

Chocolate Mint Cream Delights
Substitute store-bought or homemade vanilla icing for the filling and beat in ¹/₂ tsp (2 mL) peppermint extract and 2 to 3 drops green food coloring.

Preheat oven to 400°F (200°C)
Lightly greased cookie sheet
Round cookie cutter

1. In a bowl, sift together flour, baking powder and salt.

2. In another bowl, beat shortening and sugar until smooth and creamy. Beat in eggs, one at a time, until incorporated. Stir in vanilla and chocolate. Gradually add flour mixture, mixing until a soft dough forms. Cover tightly and refrigerate for 1 to 2 hours or overnight.

3. On a lightly floured surface, roll out dough to ¹/₈-inch (0.25-cm) thickness. Using a round cookie cutter or a glass dipped in flour, about 2 inches (5 cm) in diameter, cut out cookies and place about 2 inches (5 cm) apart on prepared cookie sheet. Sprinkle generously with sugar and bake in preheated oven for 6 to 8 minutes until cookies are set. Immediately transfer to wire racks to cool.

4. To make Filling: In a bowl, beat butter and confectioner's sugar until smooth and creamy. Beat in egg yolks and vanilla until well blended.

5. On a work surface, spread filling on one cookie then top with another to make a sandwich.

Makes 18 to 24 sandwiches

Chocolate Cream Puff Cookies

1/4 cup	butter or margarine	50 mL
1/2 cup	water	125 mL
Pinch	salt	Pinch
1/2 cup	all-purpose flour	125 mL
2	eggs	2
2 tbsp	orange zest	25 mL

Chocolate Cream Filling

1/2 cup	semi-sweet chocolate chips	125 mL
2 tbsp	orange juice	25 mL
1/3 cup	finely chopped almonds	75 mL
1/2 cup	whipping cream, whipped	125 mL
	Melted semi-sweet chocolate (optional)	

HINT: Use your slow cooker to melt chocolate in bulk and keep it warm as long as you need to. Break chocolate into chunks or 1-oz (28-g) pieces and turn to Low. Stir occasionally until melted.

Preheat oven to 450°F (230°C)
Ungreased cookie sheet

1. In a saucepan, over medium heat, bring butter, water and salt to a boil, stirring constantly. Quickly add flour and stir rapidly until mixture leaves the pan and forms a smooth ball. Remove from heat. Beat in eggs, one at a time, until incorporated. Stir in orange zest.

2. Drop batter by level teaspoonfuls (5 mL), about 2 inches (5 cm) apart, onto cookie sheet. Bake in preheated oven for 12 to 15 minutes. Immediately transfer to wire racks to cool.

3. To make Filling: In a saucepan, over low heat, melt chocolate chips. Stir in orange juice, remove from heat and allow to cool. Fold in almonds and whipped cream.

4. Using a sharp knife, cut puffs in half horizontally. Fill bottom with filling, then top. Drizzle melted chocolate over the tops, if desired. Refrigerate until ready to serve.

Makes about 4 dozen puffs

Chocolate-Filled Meringues

2	egg whites, room temperature	2
Pinch	salt	Pinch
1/2 tsp	vanilla	2 mL
1/2 cup	granulated sugar	125 mL
1	square (1 oz/28 g) bittersweet chocolate, melted (see page 11)	1

Preheat oven to 250°F (120°C)
Cookie sheet lined with parchment or foil

1. In a bowl, beat egg whites, salt and vanilla until frothy. Gradually add sugar, 2 tbsp (25 mL) at a time, beating until stiff, glossy peaks form.

2. Drop by level teaspoonfuls (5 mL), about 2 inches (5 cm) apart, onto prepared cookie sheet and using a spatula lightly flatten the tops. Bake in preheated oven for 40 to 45 minutes until meringue is crisp. Immediately transfer cookies and liner to a wire rack. When completely cool, remove meringues from liner.

3. Spread chocolate over the bottom of one meringue and top with the bottom of another to form a sandwich.

Makes about 2 dozen sandwiches

Jam-Filled Cottage Cheese Squares

1 cup	softened margarine	250 mL
1 cup	cottage cheese	250 mL
1/4 tsp	baking powder	1 mL
2 cups	all-purpose flour	500 mL
	Strawberry jam or red jelly	

Preheat oven to 425°F (220°C)
Lightly greased baking sheet
Square cookie cutter

1. In a bowl, beat margarine and cottage cheese until well combined. Stir in baking powder and flour and mix well.

2. Shape dough into a ball, wrap tightly in plastic wrap and refrigerate for 1 hour.

3. On a floured surface, divide dough in half. Roll each half into a rectangle 1/8 inch (0.25 cm) thick. Cut into 2 1/2-inch (6-cm) squares. Place a scant teaspoon (5 mL) jam in the center of each square. Fold corners up to center to make an envelope, pressing all edges together. Place about 2 inches (5 cm) apart on prepared baking sheet. Bake in preheated oven for 12 to 15 minutes until golden brown. Immediately transfer to wire racks to cool.

Makes about 4 dozen

Jam-Filled Sandwiches

2/3 cup	all-purpose flour	160 mL
3/4 tsp	baking soda	4 mL
1/2 tsp	cinnamon	2 mL
3/4 cup	softened butter	175 mL
1/2 cup	granulated sugar	125 mL
1 cup	lightly packed brown sugar	250 mL
1	egg	1
2 tsp	vanilla	10 mL
2 tbsp	water	25 mL
3 cups	rolled oats	750 mL
1 1/2 cups	raspberry jam	375 mL

Preheat oven to 350°F (180°C)
Greased cookie sheets

1. In a bowl, mix together flour, baking soda and cinnamon.

2. In another bowl, beat butter and sugars until smooth and creamy. Add egg and beat until incorporated. Stir in vanilla and water. Gradually add flour mixture beating until well blended. Stir in oats.

3. Drop by level teaspoonfuls (5 mL), about 2 inches (5 cm) apart, onto prepared cookie sheets. Bake in preheated oven for 10 to 12 minutes until golden brown. Immediately transfer to wire racks to cool. When cooled, spread with jam on the smooth side of one cookie and top with the smooth side of another cookie to form a sandwich.

Makes about 2 1/2 dozen sandwiches

Date-Filled Cookies

1³/₄ cups	all-purpose flour	425 mL
3 tsp	baking powder	15 mL
1 tsp	salt	5 mL
1 cup	softened shortening	250 mL
1 cup	lightly packed brown sugar	250 mL
¹/₂ cup	milk	125 mL
2 cups	rolled oats	500 mL
Date Filling		
2 cups	chopped, pitted dates	500 mL
1 tbsp	grated orange zest	15 mL
³/₄ cup	orange juice	175 mL
¹/₃ cup	water	75 mL

Preheat oven to 325°F (160°C)
Lightly greased baking sheet
Round cookie cutter

1. In a bowl, sift flour, baking powder and salt.

2. In another bowl, beat shortening and brown sugar until smooth and creamy. Add milk and rolled oats and stir until well blended. Add flour mixture and mix until a soft dough forms. Wrap tightly in plastic wrap and refrigerate for 1 to 2 hours until firm.

3. On a floured surface, roll out dough to ¹/₈-inch (0.25-cm) thickness. Using a cookie cutter or a glass dipped in flour, cut into rounds. Place about 2 inches (5 cm) apart on prepared cookie sheet. Bake in preheated oven for 12 to 15 minutes until golden brown. Immediately transfer to wire racks to cool.

4. To make Date Filling: In a saucepan, over medium heat, bring dates, zest, juice and water to a boil, stirring constantly. Reduce heat to low, cover and simmer, stirring occasionally, for 40 to 50 minutes until dates are very soft. Remove cover and cook, stirring for 5 minutes, until mixture becomes a thick paste. Cool completely. Spread filling over the smooth side of a cooled cookie and top with the smooth side of another cookie to form a sandwich.

Makes about 2 dozen sandwiches, depending on size of rounds

Lemon–Filled Drops

2 cups	all-purpose flour	500 mL
1/4 tsp	salt	1 mL
1 cup	softened butter or margarine	250 mL
1/2 cup	confectioner's (icing) sugar, sifted	125 mL
1 tsp	lemon extract	5 mL
	Confectioner's (icing) sugar for sprinkling	
Filling		
1/4 cup	granulated sugar	50 mL
2 1/4 tsp	cornstarch	11 mL
1 tbsp	butter or margarine	15 mL
1 tsp	grated lemon zest	5 mL
4 tsp	lemon juice	20 mL
1/4 cup	water	50 mL

Preheat oven to 400°F (200°C)
Ungreased cookie sheet

1. In a bowl, mix together flour and salt.

2. In another bowl, beat butter or margarine and confectioner's sugar until smooth and creamy. Stir in lemon extract. Add dry ingredients and mix until a soft dough forms. Cover tightly and refrigerate for 1 to 2 hours until firm.

3. Shape dough into 1-inch (2.5-cm) balls and place about 2 inches (5 cm) apart on cookie sheet. Flatten slightly with the bottom of a glass dipped in granulated sugar. Bake in preheated oven for 8 to 10 minutes until lightly browned. Immediately transfer to wire racks to cool.

4. To make Filling: In a saucepan, combine sugar and cornstarch. Add butter or margarine, lemon zest, lemon juice and water. Cook, over medium heat, stirring constantly, until mixture comes to a boil. Boil until mixture thickens, about 1 minute. Set aside to cool.

5. Spread filling over the smooth side of a cooled cookie and top with the smooth side of another cookie to form a sandwich. Sprinkle with confectioner's sugar.

Makes about 2 dozen sandwiches

Lemon Raisin-Filled Squares

1	package (8 oz/250 g) softened cream cheese	1
1/4 cup	softened butter or margarine	50 mL
1	egg	1
1/4 tsp	vanilla	1 mL
1	package (18 1/4 oz/515 g) lemon cake mix	1
Raisin Filling		
1/2 cup	raisins	125 mL
2 tbsp	water	25 mL
1/4 cup	apricot preserves	50 mL

Preheat oven to 375°F (190°C)
Ungreased cookie sheet
Square cookie cutter

1. In a bowl, beat cream cheese and butter or margarine until smooth. Beat in egg until incorporated. Stir in vanilla. Gradually add cake mix, mixing well after each addition, until a stiff dough forms.

2. Wrap dough tightly in plastic wrap and refrigerate for 30 minutes until chilled. On a floured surface, roll out dough to 1/8-inch (0.25-cm) thickness. Using a square cookie cutter, cut out shapes.

3. To make Raisin Filling: In a saucepan, over medium heat, bring raisins, water and apricot preserves to a boil. Reduce heat to low and simmer until mixture combines, about 5 minutes. Set aside to cool.

4. Place half the squares about 2 inches (5 cm) apart on cookie sheet and spoon 1/2 tsp (2 mL) filling on the center of each. Using a sharp knife, cut a 1/2 inch (1 cm) "X" in the center of the remaining squares and place on top of the squares with filling. Press together to seal. Bake in preheated oven for 10 to 12 minutes until lightly browned.

Makes about 2 dozen sandwiches

Chocolate-Dipped Lemon Butter Cookies

1 cup	softened butter	250 mL
1/2 cup	granulated sugar	125 mL
1	egg yolk	1
1 tsp	vanilla	5 mL
2 cups	all-purpose flour	500 mL
Lemon Filling		
2 cups	confectioner's (icing) sugar, sifted	500 mL
1/2 cup	softened butter	125 mL
2 tbsp	lemon juice	25 mL
Chocolate Dip		
4	squares (each 1 oz/28 g) semi-sweet chocolate	4
2 tbsp	butter	25 mL
	Finely chopped nuts (optional)	

Preheat oven to 350°F (180°C)
Ungreased cookie sheet

1. In a bowl, beat butter and sugar until smooth and creamy. Beat in egg yolk until incorporated. Stir in vanilla. Gradually add flour and mix until well blended.

2. Using your hands, shape into 1-inch (2.5-cm) balls. Flatten with the bottom of a glass dipped in sugar. Place about 2 inches (5 cm) apart on cookie sheet. Bake in preheated oven for 10 to 12 minutes until firm. Immediately transfer to wire racks to cool.

3. To make Lemon Filling: Beat confectioner's sugar, butter and lemon juice until smooth and creamy. Spread filling on the flat surface of one cookie and top with the flat surface of another cookie to form a sandwich.

4. To make Chocolate Dip: In a small saucepan, melt chocolate with butter, stirring until smooth. Cool slightly then dip half of each cookie into the chocolate. Dip chocolate-coated half in nuts, if desired. Set aside on waxed paper until chocolate hardens.

Makes about 2 dozen sandwiches

Ice-Cream Sandwiches

Use any of your favorite cookies to make these yummy ice-cream sandwiches.

	oatmeal, chocolate, chocolate chip or peanut butter cookies
	ice cream, sherbet or frozen yogurt
	chopped nuts, mini chocolate chips or sprinkles (optional)

1. Place desired number of cookies on work surface, smooth side up. Spread with a generous amount of ice cream or other filling. Top with another cookie, smooth side down, to form a sandwich.

2. For an added treat, roll the edges of the cookie sandwich in chopped nuts, mini chocolate chips or sprinkles or any other type of decorations.

3. Wrap sandwiches tightly in plastic wrap and freeze until ready to serve.

Linzer Cookies

This variation on the classic Austrian Linzertorte is a particularly delectable cookie.

2¹/₂ cups	all-purpose flour	625 mL
2 tsp	cinnamon	10 mL
¹/₂ tsp	cloves	2 mL
1 tbsp	grated lemon zest	15 mL
¹/₄ tsp	salt	1 mL
1¹/₂ cups	finely ground walnuts	375 mL
1 cup	softened butter or margarine	250 mL
1 cup	confectioner's (icing) sugar, sifted	250 mL
1	egg	1
1	egg yolk	1
1 tsp	vanilla	5 mL
	Seedless raspberry jam	
	Confectioner's (icing) sugar	

Preheat oven to 350°F (180°C)
Ungreased cookie sheets
Round or star-shaped cookie cutter and smaller cookie cutter of the same shape

1. In a bowl, mix together flour, cinnamon, cloves, lemon zest, salt and walnuts.

2. In another bowl, beat butter or margarine and confectioner's sugar until smooth and creamy. Beat in egg and egg yolk until well incorporated. Stir in vanilla. Gradually add flour mixture, mixing until a soft dough forms. Cover tightly and refrigerate for 2 to 3 hours until firm.

3. On a floured surface, roll out dough to ¹/₈-inch (0.25-cm) thickness. Using a round or star-shaped cookie cutter, cut out dough. Place half the cookies on cookie sheets. Using a smaller cookie cutter of the same shape that you used above cut out centers of the remaining cookies. Bake in preheated oven for 10 to 12 minutes until edges are lightly browned. Immediately transfer to wire racks to cool.

4. Spoon about 2 tsp (10 mL) jam onto each whole cookie. Dust confectioner's sugar onto cut cookie, then place on top of cookies with jam filling to form sandwiches.

Makes about 2 dozen sandwiches

Peanut Butter Mini Turnovers

2 cups	all-purpose flour	500 mL
1 tsp	baking powder	5 mL
1/4 tsp	salt	1 mL
3/4 cup	softened shortening, butter flavored, if available	175 mL
3/4 cup	granulated sugar	175 mL
1	egg	1
1 1/2 tsp	vanilla	7 mL
Peanut Butter Filling		
1/3 cup	smooth peanut butter	75 mL
3 tbsp	confectioner's (icing) sugar, sifted	45 mL
1/4 cup	milk	50 mL
2	squares (each 1 oz/28 g) semi-sweet chocolate, melted (optional) (see page 11)	2

Preheat oven to 375°F (190°C)
Ungreased cookie sheet
3-inch (7.5-cm) round cookie cutter

1. In a bowl, mix together flour, baking powder and salt.

2. In another bowl, beat shortening and sugar until smooth and creamy. Beat in egg until incorporated. Stir in vanilla. Gradually add flour mixture, mixing until a soft dough forms.

3. Divide dough in half and wrap each piece tightly in plastic wrap. Refrigerate for 1 to 2 hours until firm.

4. To prepare Peanut Butter Filling: In a small bowl, mix together peanut butter, confectioner's sugar and milk until smooth.

5. On a lightly floured surface, roll one piece of dough out to 1/8-inch (0.25-cm) thickness. (Leave the other piece in the refrigerator while you work.) Using a 3-inch (7.5-cm) round cookie cutter dipped in flour, cut into rounds. Place half the rounds about 2 inches (5 cm) apart on cookie sheet. Spoon a rounded teaspoonful (5 mL) of filling onto the center of each and using the back of a spoon press filling slightly to flatten. Top with the remaining rounds. Using the tines of a fork, lightly press edges of cookies to seal. Repeat with remaining dough. Bake in preheated oven for 10 to 12 minutes until edges are lightly browned. Immediately transfer to wire racks to cool. When cookies are cool, drizzle melted chocolate over tops in a zigzag pattern, if desired.

Makes about 1 1/2 dozen sandwiches

Peanut Butter Jelly Sandwiches

1¼ cups	all-purpose flour	300 mL
½ tsp	baking powder	2 mL
¾ tsp	baking soda	4 mL
¼ tsp	salt	1 mL
½ cup	softened shortening	125 mL
½ cup	packed brown sugar	125 mL
½ cup	granulated sugar	125 mL
½ cup	smooth peanut butter	125 mL
1	egg	1
	Jam or jelly	

Preheat oven to 375°F (190°C)
Lightly greased cookie sheet

1. In a bowl, mix together flour, baking powder, baking soda and salt.

2. In another bowl, beat shortening and sugars until smooth and creamy. Add peanut butter and egg and mix until well blended. Add dry ingredients and mix until a soft dough forms. Cover tightly and refrigerate for 1 hour until firm.

3. Shape dough into 1-inch (2.5-cm) balls. Place about 2 inches (5 cm) apart on prepared cookie sheet. Bake in preheated oven for 10 to 12 minutes until golden brown. Immediately transfer to wire racks.

4. When cool, place half the cookies on a pan, flat side up and spread with jam. Top with remaining cookies, flat side down to form a sandwich.

Makes about 2 dozen sandwiches

Cream Cheese Shortbread Sandwiches

Turn your favorite shortbread cookies or chocolate wafers into sandwich cookies with this great filling (see Shortbread recipes, page 175).

1	package (8 oz/250 g) softened cream cheese	1
3 tbsp	granulated sugar	45 mL
2 tbsp	coffee liqueur	25 mL
½ cup	chopped walnuts	125 mL

32 shortbread cookies, round or oblong, or 32 chocolate wafers

1. In a bowl, beat cream cheese, sugar and liqueur until smooth and creamy. Fold in nuts.

2. Spread filling between two shortbread cookies or two chocolate wafers until all the cookies are used up. Refrigerate, covered, for 2 hours.

Makes about 16 sandwiches

Mincemeat Refrigerator Rounds

2³/₄ cups	all-purpose flour	675 mL
¹/₂ tsp	baking soda	2 mL
1 tsp	salt	5 mL
1 cup	softened shortening	250 mL
¹/₂ cup	granulated sugar	125 mL
¹/₂ cup	packed brown sugar	125 mL
2	eggs	2
¹/₂ cup	prepared mincemeat	125 mL
¹/₄ cup	chopped nuts	50 mL
2 tbsp	chopped maraschino cherries (optional)	25 mL

Preheat oven to 400°F (200°C)
Ungreased cookie sheet

1. In a bowl, mix together flour, baking soda and salt.

2. In another bowl, beat shortening and sugars until smooth. Beat in eggs, one at a time, until incorporated. Gradually add dry ingredients, mixing until a soft dough forms.

3. Shape dough into two rolls about 2 inches (5 cm) wide. Wrap tightly in plastic wrap and refrigerate for 3 to 4 hours until firm.

4. In a small bowl, mix together mincemeat, nuts and cherries, if using.

5. On floured surface, cut dough into slices ¹/₈ inch (0.25 cm) thick. Place half the slices about 2 inches (5 cm) apart on cookie sheet. Place a scant teaspoonful (5 mL) of the mincemeat mixture in the center of each and top with another slice. Bake in preheated oven for 8 to 10 minutes until golden brown. Immediately transfer to wire racks to cool.

Makes about 2¹/₂ dozen sandwiches

Grandma's Whoopie Pies

½ cup	cocoa powder	125 mL
½ cup	hot water (not boiling)	125 mL
2⅔ cups	all-purpose flour	660 mL
1 tsp	baking powder	5 mL
1 tsp	baking soda	5 mL
¼ tsp	salt	1 mL
½ cup	softened shortening	125 mL
1½ cups	granulated sugar	375 mL
2	eggs	2
1 tsp	vanilla	5 mL
½ cup	buttermilk	125 mL
Filling		
3 tbsp	all-purpose flour	45 mL
Pinch	salt	Pinch
1 cup	milk	250 mL
¾ cup	softened shortening	175 mL
1½ cups	confectioner's (icing) sugar, sifted	375 mL
2 tsp	vanilla	10 mL

HINT: If a recipe calls for buttermilk and you don't have any on hand, add 1 tbsp (15 mL) vinegar or lemon juice to each cup of regular milk for instant buttermilk.

Preheat oven to 350°F (180°C)
Lightly greased cookie sheet

1. In a small bowl, combine cocoa and hot water and mix well. Set aside to cool for 5 minutes.

2. In a bowl, sift together flour, baking powder, baking soda and salt.

3. In another bowl, beat shortening and sugar until smooth and creamy. Add eggs, one at a time, beating until well incorporated. Stir in vanilla. Add cocoa mixture and mix well. Add flour mixture alternately with buttermilk, mixing until thoroughly blended.

4. Drop dough by rounded teaspoonfuls (5 mL), about 2 inches (5 cm) apart, onto prepared baking sheet. Using a spoon or the palm of your hand, flatten slightly. Bake in preheated oven for 10 to 12 minutes until firm. Immediately transfer to wire racks to cool.

5. To make Filling: In a small saucepan, mix flour and salt. Slowly whisk in milk until smooth. Cook, over medium heat, stirring constantly, for 5 to 8 minutes until thick. Remove from heat, cover, and place in refrigerator to cool completely.

6. In a bowl, beat shortening, confectioner's sugar and vanilla until smooth and creamy. Add chilled mixture and beat for 5 minutes until light and fluffy.

7. On a work surface, spread filling over the flat surface of half the cookies. Top with remaining cookies, flat side down to form sandwiches. Store in the refrigerator.

Makes about 2 dozen sandwiches

Apricot Almond Sandwiches

2¹/₂ cups	all-purpose flour	625 mL
¹/₄ tsp	baking soda	1 mL
¹/₄ tsp	salt	1 mL
¹/₂ cup	softened shortening	125 mL
1 cup	granulated sugar	250 mL
2	eggs	2
1 tsp	vanilla	5 mL
Filling		
²/₃ cup	granulated sugar	160 mL
²/₃ cup	water	160 mL
1 tsp	lemon juice	5 mL
2 cups	canned apricots, mashed	500 mL
¹/₂ cup	finely chopped almonds	125 mL

Ungreased cookie sheet
Preheat oven to 375°F (190°C)
Round cookie cutter

1. In a bowl, mix together flour, baking soda and salt.

2. In another bowl, beat shortening and sugar until smooth and creamy. Beat in eggs, one at a time, until well incorporated. Stir in vanilla. Gradually add flour mixture, mixing until a soft dough forms. Cover and refrigerate for 1 to 2 hours until firm.

3. To make Filling: In a saucepan, over low heat, mix together sugar, water, lemon juice, apricots and almonds. Cook, stirring, until thickened, about 15 minutes. Set aside to cool.

4. On a floured work surface, divide dough in half. One at a time, roll out each half to ¹/₈-inch (0.25-cm) thickness. Using a round cookie cutter, cut circles in one portion and place 1-inch (2.5-cm) apart on cookie sheet. Using the same cutter, cut out the other portion then, using the open side of a thimble, or a pastry cutter make a small hole in the center 1-inch (2.5-cm) apart and place on sheet. Bake in preheated oven until edges are lightly browned. Immediately transfer to wire racks to cool. When cool, spread filling on the solid cookie and top with the cut out cookie.

Makes about 15 sandwiches

Just Peachy Sandwich Cookies

²/₃ cup	softened butter or margarine	160 mL
¹/₂ cup	confectioner's (icing) sugar, sifted	125 mL
2 tsp	grated lemon zest	10 mL
¹/₂ tsp	nutmeg	2 mL
1³/₄ cups	all-purpose flour	425 mL
Peach Filling		
¹/₂ cup	peach preserves	125 mL
1 tbsp	granulated sugar	15 mL

HINT: Drop a bay leaf into your sugar and flour canisters to keep unwanted pests away. It does not change the taste.

Preheat oven to 325°F (160°C)
Ungreased cookie sheet

1. In a bowl, beat butter or margarine, confectioner's sugar, lemon zest and nutmeg until smooth and creamy. Gradually stir in flour, until thoroughly blended.

2. Shape dough into 1-inch (2.5-cm) balls and place 2 inches (5 cm) apart on cookie sheet. Using the bottom of a glass or the tines of a fork dipped in sugar flatten slightly. Bake in preheated oven for 12 to 15 minutes until golden brown. Immediately transfer to wire racks to cool.

3. To make Peach Filling: In a small saucepan, over low heat, bring preserves and sugar to a boil, stirring constantly. Cook, stirring, for 2 minutes until sugar dissolves and mixture is syrupy. Remove from heat and set aside to cool completely.

4. On a work surface, place half the cookies, flat side up. Spread each with about ¹/₂ tsp (2 mL) of the filling. Top with remaining cookies, flat side down, to form a sandwich. Press together gently. Dab any leftover filling on top of each sandwich as a garnish.

Makes 2 dozen sandwiches

Lacy Oatmeal Sandwiches

$2/3$ cup	all-purpose flour	160 mL
2 cups	quick oats	500 mL
$2/3$ cup	butter or margarine, melted	160 mL
1 cup	granulated sugar	250 mL
$1/4$ cup	corn syrup	50 mL
$1/4$ cup	milk	50 mL
Filling		
1 cup	semi-sweet chocolate chips, melted	250 mL
1 cup	white chocolate chips, melted	250 mL

NOTE: Drizzle any leftover chocolate over the tops of the cookies for added decoration.

Preheat oven to 375°F (190°C)
Cookie sheet lined with buttered foil

1. In a bowl, mix together flour and oats.

2. In another bowl, mix together butter or margarine, sugar and corn syrup. Add milk and mix well. Stir in flour mixture and mix thoroughly.

3. Drop batter by level teaspoonfuls (5 mL), about 3 inches (7.5 cm) apart, onto prepared cookie sheet and using the back of a spoon or the tines of a fork press down slightly on each. Bake in preheated oven for 8 to 10 minutes until cookies have spread and are browned around the edges. Immediately transfer foil and cookies to wire racks. When cool peel cookies off the foil.

4. On a work surface, spread a thin layer of semi-sweet chocolate on the bottom of some cookies and white chocolate on others. Top each with the bottom side of remaining cookies.

Makes about 2 dozen sandwiches

No-Bake Cookies

What could be easier than making cookies that you don't even have to bake? Some of these tasty treats require a bit of stovetop cooking, others are just mixed, shaped and chilled. All are simple, failproof, fun and delicious.

Almond–Coated Chocolate Fig Balls

2³/₄ cups	trimmed dried figs	675 mL
¹/₄ cup	water	50 mL
¹/₂ cup	bourbon, divided	125 mL
3¹/₄ cups	crushed vanilla wafers, about 68 cookies	800 mL
1 cup	confectioner's (icing) sugar, sifted	250 mL
1 cup	ground almonds or pecans, divided	250 mL
3 tbsp	all-purpose flour	45 mL
¹/₄ tsp	cinnamon	1 mL
1 cup	mini chocolate chips	250 mL
2 tbsp	light corn syrup	25 mL
¹/₄ cup	granulated sugar	50 mL

Food processor
Airtight container

1. In a saucepan, combine figs, water and ¹/₄ cup (50 mL) bourbon. Bring to a boil over low heat, then simmer, covered, for 10 minutes. Set aside to cool.

2. In a bowl, mix together vanilla wafers, confectioner's sugar, ¹/₂ cup (125 mL) ground pecans, flour, cinnamon and chocolate chips.

3. In a food processor, combine cooled fig mixture, corn syrup and remaining bourbon. Process until figs are puréed and mixture is smooth. Add to vanilla wafer mixture and mix until blended.

4. In a small bowl, mix remaining ¹/₂ cup (125 mL) ground almonds or pecans with granulated sugar.

5. Shape dough into 1-inch (2.5-cm) balls, then roll in the sugar-nut mixture. Place in an airtight container and allow to mellow for at least 24 hours.

Makes about 4 dozen

No–Bake Granola Peanut Treats

6 cups	miniature marshmallows	1.5 L
¹/₄ cup	butter or margarine	50 mL
¹/₂ cup	smooth or crunchy peanut butter	125 mL
4 cups	granola cereal	1 L
1 cup	semi-sweet chocolate chips	250 mL

Large platter or cookie sheet lined with waxed paper

1. In a saucepan, over low heat, melt marshmallows and butter or margarine, stirring until mixture is smooth. Remove from heat. Add peanut butter and mix well. Stir in granola and chocolate chips.

2. Shape mixture into 1-inch (2.5-cm) balls and place on platter or prepared cookie sheet. Refrigerate until firm.

Makes about 3 dozen

Cranberry Pistachio Biscotti (page 93)

Homemade Ladyfingers (page 104)

Delicate Lace Baskets (page 109)

Ice-Cream Sandwiches (page 118)

Lacy Oatmeal Sandwiches (page 126)

Peppermint Candy Canes (page 159)
Checkerboard Squares (page 162)

Cream Cheese Shortbread (page 180)

Original Scottish Shortbread (page 160)

Chocolate Haystacks

6	squares (each 1 oz/28 g) semi-sweet chocolate	6	
1 cup	mini butterscotch chips	250 mL	
2 cups	dried chow mein noodles	500 mL	
1 cup	salted peanuts	250 mL	
1 cup	miniature marshmallows	250 mL	

Large platter or cookie sheet lined with waxed paper

1. In the top of a double boiler, over hot water, melt chocolate and butterscotch chips, stirring constantly until smooth.

2. Add noodles, peanuts and marshmallows, stirring until well coated with chocolate mixture.

3. Drop by rounded teaspoonfuls (5 mL) onto platter or prepared cookie sheet. Refrigerate until firm.

Makes about 3 dozen

Crispy Caramel Haystacks

2½ cups	miniature marshmallows	625 mL	
3 tbsp	butter or margarine	45 mL	
2 cups	dried chow mein noodles	500 mL	
12	caramels	12	
1 tbsp	water	15 mL	
2 tbsp	smooth or crunchy peanut butter	25 mL	

Large platter or cookie sheet lined with waxed paper

1. In a large saucepan, over low heat, melt marshmallows and butter or margarine, stirring constantly until smooth. Add noodles and stir until well coated.

2. Drop mixture by teaspoonfuls (5 mL) onto platter or prepared cookie sheet.

3. In a saucepan, over low heat, melt caramels in water, stirring until smooth. Add peanut butter and mix well. Drizzle caramel mixture over haystacks. Refrigerate until firm.

Makes about 2 dozen

No-Bake Peanut Butter-Rice Chews

²/₃ cup	corn syrup	160 mL
²/₃ cup	smooth peanut butter	160 mL
¹/₂ cup	lightly packed brown sugar	125 mL
2¹/₂ cups	crisp rice cereal	625 mL
1 cup	shredded coconut	250 mL
¹/₂ cup	chopped nuts	125 mL

HINT: To ease clean-up when measuring 1-cup (250-mL) quantities of messy ingredients such as honey or syrup, use 8 oz (250 mL) paper cups in place of glass measuring cups. When through, just throw them away.

Large platter or cookie sheet lined with waxed paper

1. In a large saucepan, over low heat, combine corn syrup, peanut butter and brown sugar, stirring constantly, until sugar is dissolved. Remove from heat. Stir in rice cereal, coconut and nuts until thoroughly blended.

2. Drop mixture by tablespoonfuls (15 mL) onto prepared cookie sheet and refrigerate until firm.

Makes about 3 dozen

Barnyard Cow Pies

2 cups	milk chocolate chips	500 mL
1 tbsp	shortening	15 mL
¹/₂ cup	raisins	125 mL
¹/₂ cup	chopped slivered almonds	125 mL

Large platter or cookie sheet lined with waxed paper

1. In the top of a double boiler, over hot water, melt chocolate chips with shortening, stirring constantly until smooth. Remove from heat. Stir in raisins and almonds until well blended.

2. Drop by tablespoonfuls (15 mL) onto platter or prepared cookie sheet and refrigerate until firm.

Makes about 2 dozen

Chocolate Rum Balls

1 cup	vanilla wafer crumbs	250 mL
1¹/₂ cups	chopped pecans	375 mL
1 cup	confectioner's (icing) sugar, sifted	250 mL
¹/₄ cup	unsweetened cocoa	50 mL
2 tbsp	corn syrup	25 mL
¹/₄ cup	dark rum	50 mL
¹/₂ cup	fine granulated sugar	125 mL

Airtight container

1. In a bowl, mix together wafer crumbs, pecans, confectioner's sugar and cocoa. Stir in syrup and rum until well blended.

2. Shape dough into 1-inch (2.5-cm) balls and roll in sugar. Store in tightly covered container.

Makes 2¹/₂ dozen

No-Bake Cocoa Orange Balls

¹/₄ cup	unsweetened cocoa, sifted	50 mL
1 cup	confectioner's (icing) sugar, sifted	250 mL
1 cup	graham wafer crumbs, about 14 crackers	250 mL
2 tbsp	corn syrup	25 mL
1 tsp	vanilla	5 mL
¹/₄ cup	frozen orange juice concentrate, thawed and undiluted	50 mL
	Cocoa or confectioner's sugar for coating	

Small baking cups (optional)

1. In a bowl, mix together cocoa, confectioner's sugar and graham wafer crumbs. Make a well in the center.

2. In another bowl, combine corn syrup, vanilla and orange juice concentrate. Add to cocoa mixture and stir until blended. Cover and refrigerate for 30 minutes.

3. Shape mixture into 1-inch (2.5-cm) balls and roll in cocoa or confectioner's sugar. Place in baking cups for decoration, if desired. Store in the refrigerator, but bring to room temperature before serving.

Makes about 2¹/₂ dozen

Chocolate Covered Peanut Graham Balls

3 tbsp	softened butter	45 mL
¹/₂ cup	smooth peanut butter	125 mL
1 cup	confectioner's (icing) sugar, sifted	250 mL
1 cup	graham wafer crumbs	250 mL
8	squares (each 1 oz/28 g) semi-sweet chocolate, melted (see page 11)	8

Large platter or cookie sheet lined with waxed paper

1. In a bowl, beat butter, peanut butter and confectioner's sugar until smooth. Add wafer crumbs and mix until well blended.

2. Shape mixture into 1-inch (2.5-cm) balls and place on platter or prepared cookie sheet. Refrigerate 30 minutes until firm.

3. Using a spoon or your fingers, dip balls in melted chocolate and roll around until all surfaces are covered. Return to cookie sheet and refrigerate until chocolate sets. Store, tightly covered in refrigerator.

Makes about 2 dozen

Pineapple Snowballs

1	package (4 oz/125 g) softened cream cheese	1
2½ cups	confectioner's (icing) sugar, sifted	625 mL
1 cup	vanilla wafer crumbs	250 mL
¼ tsp	salt	1 mL
½ cup	crushed pineapple, drained	125 mL
½ cup	quartered miniature marshmallows	125 mL
	Shredded coconut	

Large platter or cookie sheet lined with waxed paper

1. In a bowl, beat cream cheese until smooth. Gradually add confectioner's sugar, mixing until creamy. Stir in wafer crumbs and salt and mix well. Add pineapple, then marshmallows, stirring until well combined. Cover bowl with plastic wrap and refrigerate for 1 hour.

2. Shape mixture into 1-inch (2.5-cm) balls and roll in coconut until well coated. Place on platter or prepared cookie sheet and refrigerate until firm.

Makes about 3 dozen

Fruit 'n' Nut Snowballs

4 cups	All-Bran cereal	1 L
1 cup	pitted dried prunes	250 mL
1⅔ cups	raisins	410 mL
1½ cups	dried apricots	375 mL
2 cups	chopped pecans	500 mL
	Confectioner's (icing) sugar	

Food processor
Airtight container

1. Place cereal and prunes in a food processor and process until cereal is crumbled. Add raisins, apricots and pecans and process until fruit is finely chopped.

2. Shape mixture into 1-inch (2.5-cm) balls, then roll in confectioner's sugar. Store in a tightly covered container. Before serving, roll again in confectioner's sugar.

Makes about 5 dozen

HINT: To keep dried fruit fresh after the package has been opened, place in an airtight container and refrigerate. To soften hardened fruit, soak in hot water or juice.

Rocky Road Specials

8	squares (each 1 oz/28 g) semi-sweet chocolate	8
1 cup	miniature marshmallows	250 mL
1 cup	chopped walnuts	250 mL
1/3 cup	white chocolate, coarsely chopped, about 2 oz (56 g)	75 mL

HINT: To freshen up stale marshmallows, store them in an airtight container with a slice of fresh bread.

Large platter or cookie sheet lined with waxed paper

1. In top of a double boiler, over hot water, melt semi-sweet chocolate, stirring occasionally until smooth. Remove pot from hot water and let stand for 10 to 15 minutes until chocolate has cooled slightly. Stir in marshmallows, walnuts and white chocolate until well blended.

2. Drop by rounded tablespoonfuls (15 mL) onto platter or prepared cookie sheet and refrigerate until chocolate has set.

Makes about 2 dozen

Stovetop Cookies

1/2 cup	chopped dates	125 mL
2	eggs, beaten	2
3/4 cup	granulated sugar	175 mL
1 tsp	vanilla	5 mL
Pinch	salt	Pinch
1 cup	crisp rice cereal	250 mL
1 cup	coarsely crushed cornflakes	250 mL
	Flaked or shredded coconut	

HINT: To color coconut, add food coloring to 1 tsp (5 mL) water and toss the coconut until evenly colored.

1. In a heavy frying pan, over low heat, stirring constantly, cook dates, eggs and sugar for 8 minutes. Remove from heat. Stir in vanilla and salt, then rice cereal and cornflakes. Mix together until well blended.

2. Wet hands and roll dough into balls or fingers. On a plate, roll balls in coconut until well coated.

Makes about 2 dozen

Stovetop Sugarplum Gems

¹/₂ cup	cooking dates, cut into thin strips	125 mL
¹/₂ cup	dried apricots, cut into thin strips	125 mL
3 tbsp	water	45 mL
2 tbsp	liquid honey	25 mL
2 tbsp	orange juice	25 mL
1 tsp	grated orange zest	5 mL
¹/₄ cup	finely chopped pecans	50 mL
³/₄ cup	shredded coconut	175 mL
	Confectioner's (icing) sugar	

HINT: If shredded or flaked coconut dries out, sprinkle with milk and let stand until it softens to the desired consistency. If you won't be using coconut for awhile, to prevent it from becoming moldy, toast in a skillet, then store.

Food processor
Large platter or cookie sheet lined with waxed paper

1. In a saucepan, combine dates, apricots, water, honey and orange juice. Cover and cook over medium heat until simmering. Reduce heat to low and stirring constantly, cook for 10 minutes until fruit is very tender and liquid has evaporated. (If liquid evaporates before the fruit softens, add about 1 tbsp (15 mL) water.) Remove from heat and set aside until mixture is lukewarm, then process in a food processor until mixture is a fairly smooth paste.

2. Transfer mixture to a bowl and stir in orange zest and pecans, mixing until well blended.

3. Spread coconut out on a shallow dish. Pinch off a rounded teaspoonful (5 mL) of dough and using the palms of your hands roll into a ball. Drop into coconut and roll until well coated. Repeat with remaining dough.

4. Place on platter or prepared cookie sheet and sprinkle with confectioner's sugar.

Makes about 2¹/₂ dozen

Esther's Favorites

This chapter is a tribute to my family and friends who have provided me with so many wonderful cookie recipes over the years.

Mama's Homemade Cookies

4 cups	all-purpose flour	1 L
1 tsp	baking soda	5 mL
1/4 tsp	salt	1 mL
3	eggs	3
1/2 cup	vegetable oil	125 mL
1 cup	granulated sugar	250 mL
1 tsp	vanilla	5 mL
1/2 cup	milk	125 mL

Preheat oven to 350°F (180°C)
Ungreased cookie sheet

1. In a bowl, mix together flour, baking soda and salt. Make a well in the center.

2. In a separate bowl, whisk together eggs, oil, sugar, vanilla and milk. Pour mixture into well and mix thoroughly.

3. Drop by rounded teaspoonfuls (5 mL), 2 inches (5 cm) apart, onto cookie sheet. Bake in preheated oven for about 20 minutes or until golden brown. Immediately transfer to wire racks to cool.

Makes about 5 dozen

Cecille's One-Bowl Chocolate Cookies

16	squares (each 1 oz/28 g) semi-sweet chocolate, divided	16
3/4 cup	firmly packed brown sugar	175 mL
1/4 cup	softened butter or margarine	50 mL
2	eggs	2
1 tsp	vanilla	5 mL
1/4 tsp	baking powder	1 mL
1/2 cup	all-purpose flour	125 mL
2 cups	chopped nuts (optional)	500 mL

HINT: If you do not have enough cookie sheets when baking cookies, use a baking pan instead. Turn it over and set the cookies on the bottom.

Preheat oven to 350°F (180°C)
Ungreased cookie sheet

1. Coarsely chop half of the chocolate and set aside.

2. In a large bowl, in a microwave oven, melt remaining chocolate (see page 11). Add brown sugar, butter, eggs and vanilla, beating until smooth. Stir in baking powder, then flour and mix until well blended. Fold in reserved chocolate and nuts, if using, mixing until well combined.

3. Using a 1/4 cup (50 mL) measure, drop by cupfuls onto cookie sheet. Bake in preheated oven for 12 to 13 minutes until cookies are puffed and soft to touch. Cool on cookie sheet for 1 minute, then transfer to wire racks to cool completely.

Makes about 1 1/2 dozen large cookies

Lisa's Chocolate Chip Cookies

1 cup	all-purpose flour	250 mL
1/2 tsp	baking soda	2 mL
1/2 tsp	salt	2 mL
1/2 cup	softened shortening or butter	125 mL
1/2 cup	granulated sugar	125 mL
1/4 cup	firmly packed brown sugar	50 mL
1	egg	1
1 tsp	vanilla	5 mL
1	package (10 oz/300 g) mini chocolate chips	1

Preheat oven to 375°F (190°C)
Ungreased cookie sheet

1. In a bowl, mix together flour, baking soda and salt.

2. In another bowl, beat shortening or butter and sugars until smooth and creamy. Beat in egg until incorporated. Stir in vanilla. Fold in chocolate chips. Add flour mixture and mix thoroughly.

3. Drop by rounded teaspoonfuls (5 mL), about 2 inches (5 cm) apart, onto cookie sheet. Bake in preheated oven for 8 to 10 minutes or until lightly browned. Immediately transfer to wire racks to cool.

Makes about 2 dozen

Shirley's Meringue Cookies

1/2 cup	granulated sugar	125 mL
3 tbsp	potato flour or cornstarch	45 mL
3	egg whites	3
1 cup	chocolate chips	250 mL

NOTE: Potato flour is available in the baking section of supermarkets.

HINT: Don't beat egg whites in plastic bowls as they retain oils. Use a very clean bowl with no traces of oil.

VARIATION

Coconut Meringues
Substitute 1 cup (250 mL) sweetened, shredded coconut for the chocolate chips.

Preheat oven to 250°F (120°C)
Cookie sheet lined with waxed paper

1. In a bowl, mix together sugar and potato flour or cornstarch.

2. In another bowl, beat egg whites until soft peaks form. Gradually add sugar mixture to egg whites, beating until stiff, glossy peaks form. Fold in chocolate chips.

3. Drop by teaspoonfuls (5 mL), about 2 inches (5 cm) apart, onto prepared cookie sheet. Bake in preheated oven for 55 to 60 minutes until lightly browned. Immediately transfer to wire racks to cool.

Makes about 2 dozen

Baba Mary's Jam Delights

2 cups	all-purpose flour	500 mL
2 tsp	baking powder	10 mL
Pinch	salt	Pinch
3/4 cup	shortening	175 mL
1/2 cup	granulated sugar	125 mL
2	eggs	2
	Jam for filling, any flavor	

Preheat oven to 350°F (180°C)
Cookie sheets lined with parchment or waxed paper

1. In a bowl, sift together flour, baking powder and salt.

2. In another bowl, beat shortening and sugar until smooth and creamy. Add eggs, one at a time, beating after each addition. Gradually mix in flour mixture until well blended.

3. Shape dough into 1-inch (2.5-cm) balls. Using a thimble or your thumb make an indentation in the center of each cookie and fill with jam. Bake in preheated oven for 15 minutes until golden brown. Immediately transfer to wire racks to cool.

Makes about 4 dozen

Shauna's Shortbread Cookies

1 1/2 cups	sifted pastry flour	375 mL
1/2 cup	cornstarch	125 mL
1/2 tsp	salt	2 mL
1/2 lb	softened butter	250 g
2/3 cup	lightly packed brown sugar	160 mL
1/2 cup	glazed cherries (optional)	125 mL
1/2 cup	chopped almonds (optional)	125 mL

Preheat oven to 300°F (150°C)
Ungreased cookie sheet
Cookie cutter

1. In a bowl, mix together pastry flour, cornstarch and salt.

2. In another bowl, beat butter and brown sugar until smooth and creamy. Stir in cherries and almonds, if using. Gradually add flour mixture, mixing thoroughly after each addition until a soft dough forms. Knead lightly.

3. On a lightly floured board, knead dough until cracks appear on the surface. Roll out to about 1/4-inch (0.5-cm) thickness. Using a knife or a cookie cutter, cut into small oblongs and place on cookie sheet. Bake in preheated oven for 20 to 25 minutes or until golden brown. Immediately transfer to wire racks to cool.

Makes about 2 dozen

Aunty Giza's Lemon Cookies

1³/₄ cups	all-purpose flour	325 mL
1 tsp	baking powder	5 mL
¹/₄ tsp	salt	1 mL
¹/₄ lb	softened shortening	125 g
³/₄ cup	granulated sugar	175 mL
2	egg yolks	2
	Zest and juice of ¹/₂ lemon	
¹/₂ cup	orange juice	125 mL
2 tsp	red wine (optional)	10 mL
	Egg whites	
	Halved nuts (optional)	

HINT: Leftover egg yolks or whites can be kept in the refrigerator for 3 to 4 days in airtight containers. Yolks should be covered with cold water to keep them from drying up.

Preheat oven to 350°F (180°C)
Lightly greased cookie sheet

1. In a bowl, mix together, flour, baking powder and salt.

2. In another bowl, beat shortening and sugar until smooth and creamy. Beat in egg yolks until incorporated. Stir in lemon zest and juice, orange juice and wine, if using. Add flour mixture and mix until a dough forms.

3. Cut dough in half. Shape into 1-inch (2.5-cm) balls and using your finger, press down on each to flatten slightly. Place about 1-inch (2.5-cm) apart on prepared cookie sheet. Brush egg white on top of each cookie and place a nut, if desired, in the center. Bake in preheated oven for 20 minutes until golden brown. Immediately transfer to wire racks to cool.

Makes about 4 dozen

Mom's Peanut Butter Cookies

1 cup	all-purpose flour	250 mL
1 tsp	baking soda	5 mL
¹/₄ tsp	salt	1 mL
¹/₂ cup	softened shortening	125 mL
¹/₂ cup	granulated sugar	125 mL
¹/₂ cup	lightly packed brown sugar	125 mL
1	egg	1
¹/₂ cup	smooth peanut butter or crunchy style, if desired	125 mL
¹/₄ tsp	vanilla	1 mL

Preheat oven to 350°F (180°C)
Lightly greased cookie sheet

1. In a bowl, mix together flour, baking soda and salt.

2. In another bowl, beat shortening and sugars until smooth and creamy. Beat in egg until incorporated. Stir in peanut butter and vanilla. Gradually add flour mixture, mixing until a soft dough forms.

3. Shape dough into 1-inch (2.5-cm) balls. Place about 2 inches (5 cm) apart on prepared cookie sheet and using the tines of a fork press to flatten. Bake in preheated oven for 12 to 15 minutes. Immediately transfer to wire racks to cool.

Makes about 2 dozen

Esther's Famous Komish Bread Cookies

I also refer to these as Chocolate Chip Miniscotti. They are the favorite cookies of my son Leonard and daughter Lisa. Vary the quantity of cinnamon, according to your taste. I probably use more than most people, as I love cinnamon.

3 cups	all-purpose flour	750 mL
1/2 tsp	salt	2 mL
1 tsp	baking powder	5 mL
1 to 2 tsp	cinnamon	5 to 10 mL
3	eggs	3
1 cup	granulated sugar	250 mL
1 cup	oil	250 mL
1 tsp	vanilla	5 mL
1 cup	chocolate chips	250 mL

Sugar–Cinnamon Mix

1/2 cup	granulated sugar	125 mL
2 tsp	ground cinnamon	10 mL

Preheat oven to 350°F (180°C)
Greased cookie sheet

1. In a bowl, mix together flour, salt, baking powder and cinnamon.

2. In another bowl, beat eggs, sugar and oil until blended. Mix in vanilla. Add dry ingredients and mix well. Fold in chocolate chips.

3. On a floured surface, divide dough into three portions. Shape into three rolls about 2 to 3 inches (5 to 7.5 cm) wide. Place at least 2 inches (5 cm) apart on prepared cookie sheet. Bake in preheated oven for 30 to 35 minutes until lightly browned and a toothpick inserted into center of one of the rolls comes out clean and dry. Remove from oven and turn off heat.

4. To make Sugar-Cinnamon Mix: In a small bowl, mix sugar and cinnamon.

5. On a cutting board, cut hot rolls into slices about 1/2 inch (1 cm) thick. Dip each slice in sugar-cinnamon mix until well coated. Place on cookie sheet, and leaving heat off, return to oven to dry for 20 to 25 minutes.

Makes about 4 dozen

Lisa's Cinnamon Nut Crescents

Compared to other cookies, these are a lot of work. But they are definitely worth it.

1	package (¹/₄ oz/8 g) active dry yeast	1
³/₄ cup + 2 tbsp	granulated sugar, divided	175 mL + 25 mL
¹/₂ cup	warm water	125 mL
3 cups	all-purpose flour	750 mL
¹/₂ tsp	salt	2 mL
3	egg yolks	3
¹/₂ cup	whipping cream	125 mL
1 tsp	vanilla	5 mL
1 cup	softened butter or margarine	250 mL
Filling		
2	egg whites	2
1³/₄ cups	finely chopped walnuts, toasted (see page 11)	425 mL
³/₄ cup	granulated sugar	175 mL
Pinch	salt	Pinch
Sugar–Cinnamon Mix		
³/₄ cup	granulated sugar	175 mL
3 tbsp	cinnamon	45 mL

Preheat oven to 350°F (180°C)
Greased foil–lined cookie sheets

1. In a bowl, dissolve yeast and 2 tbsp (25 mL) sugar in warm water.

2. In another bowl, combine flour and salt. Add yeast mixture, mixing until blended, then mix in egg yolks, cream and vanilla. Beat in butter, spoonfuls at a time, until well blended and a dough forms. Wrap tightly in plastic wrap and refrigerate for at least 3 hours or overnight until dough is firm.

3. To make Filling: In a bowl, beat egg whites until soft peaks form. Fold in walnuts, remaining ³/₄ cup (175 mL) sugar and salt. Set aside.

4. To make Sugar-Cinnamon Mix: In a small bowl, mix sugar and cinnamon.

5. Divide dough into 10 balls and return nine to refrigerator until ready to use. On a work surface, sprinkled with a heaping table-spoonful (15 mL) sugar-cinnamon mixture, roll one dough ball into an 8-inch (20-cm) circle, turning at least once so both sides will be coated with the sugar-cinnamon mixture. Using a knife or a pastry cutter, fluted, if desired, cut into eight pie-shaped wedges. Place 1 tsp (5 mL) walnut filling on the outer edge of each wedge. Beginning with the outer edge and finishing with the point in the center, roll up to form crescents. Repeat with remaining dough.

6. Place, point side down, on prepared sheets and bake in preheated oven for 12 to 15 minutes until puffy and browned. Immediately transfer to wire racks to cool.

Makes about 6 ¹/₂ dozen

Sima's Passover Cookies

2	eggs	2
1/2 cup	oil	125 mL
2 tbsp	potato starch	25 mL
1 tbsp	lemon juice	15 mL
3/4 cup	granulated sugar	175 mL
1 cup	cake meal	250 mL
3/4 cup	ground almonds, divided	175 mL
1/2 cup	sugar-cinnamon mix (see page 11)	125 mL

Preheat oven to 350°F (180°C)
Lightly greased cookie sheet

1. In a bowl, beat together eggs and oil. Add potato starch and lemon juice and mix well. Add sugar and cake meal, mixing until blended. Fold in 1/2 cup (125 mL) ground almonds.

2. Roll dough into 1-inch (2.5-cm) balls. Mix remaining 1/4 cup (50 mL) ground almonds with sugar-cinnamon mix and roll the ball in this mixture to coat. Flatten a little, if desired.

3. Place about 2 inches (5 cm) apart on prepared cookie sheet. Bake for 10 to 12 minutes until golden brown. Immediately transfer to wire racks to cool

Makes about 2 dozen

Cecille's Passover Komish Bread

3	eggs	3
3/4 cup	granulated sugar	175 mL
3/4 cup	oil	175 mL
1 to 2 tsp	cinnamon	5 to 10 mL
3/4 cup	cake meal	175 mL
1/4 cup	matzo meal	50 mL
2 tbsp	potato starch	25 mL
1/2 cup	chopped walnuts	125 mL

HINT: When you buy cooking oil, instead of removing the protective seal, cut a small slit in it. You'll be able to pour the oil through it without spilling.

Preheat oven to 325°F (160°C)
Greased 9-inch (2.5-L) square cake pan

1. In a bowl, beat eggs and sugar until thick and pale. Beat in oil until well incorporated. Add cinnamon, to taste, cake meal, matzo meal and potato starch, mixing until well blended. Fold in nuts.

2. Using a spatula, scrape batter into prepared pan and bake in preheated oven for 50 to 60 minutes until a toothpick inserted in the center comes out clean and dry. Cool in pan for 30 minutes, then cut into slices 1/2 inch (1 cm) thick. Place on wire racks.

3. Increase oven heat to 350°F (180°C) and return rack of slices to oven to dry for 30 minutes. Remove from oven and cool completely before serving.

Makes 4 1/2 dozen

Esther's Rugelach

Rugelach, tiny crescents made from a cream cheese dough, are often served during the Jewish festival of Hanukah, but many people eat them all year round.

2 cups	all-purpose flour	500 mL
1/4 cup	granulated sugar	50 mL
1 cup	softened butter (2 sticks)	250 mL
1	package (8 oz/250 g) softened cream cheese	1
Filling		
1/2 cup	granulated sugar	125 mL
1 tbsp	cinnamon	15 mL
3/4 cup	finely chopped walnuts	175 mL
1/2 cup	raisins (optional)	125 mL
1/4 cup	melted butter	50 mL

VARIATION

Raspberry–Hazelnut Rugelach
In a bowl, mix together 1/2 cup (125 mL) raspberry jam and 1/2 cup (125 mL) finely chopped toasted hazelnuts (see page 11). Spread over circle after brushing with butter. Sprinkle lightly with granulated sugar.

Preheat oven to 350°F (180°C)
Cookie sheet lined with parchment or waxed paper

1. In a bowl, mix together flour and 1/4 cup (50 mL) sugar. Using your fingers, work the butter and cream cheese together to form a dough. (You can also do this in a food processor.)

2. Divide dough into four sections. Wrap tightly in plastic wrap and refrigerate for at least 4 hours.

3. To make Filling: In a bowl, mix together 1/2 cup (125 mL) sugar, cinnamon, walnuts and raisins, if using.

4. On a floured surface, using a floured rolling pin, roll one portion of dough into a 10-inch (25-cm) circle. Brush with 1 tbsp (15 mL) melted butter, then spread one quarter of the filling evenly over circle.

5. Using a knife or a pastry wheel, cut circle into 12 pie-shaped wedges. Beginning at the wide edge, with the filling inside, roll tightly, finishing with the point in the middle. Curve the rolls slightly to form a crescent and place, point side down on prepared cookie sheet. Repeat with remaining dough.

6. Bake in preheated oven for 25 to 30 minutes until delicately browned.

Makes about 4 dozen

Mildred's Sour Cream Kiffles

1	package (¹⁄₄ oz/8 g) active dry yeast	1
6 cups	all-purpose flour	1.5 L
6 tbsp	granulated sugar	90 mL
1 tsp	salt	5 mL
1 cup	butter	250 mL
1 cup	margarine	250 mL
4	eggs, beaten	4
1 cup	sour cream	250 mL
2 cups	sugar-cinnamon mix (see page 11)	500 mL

Preheat oven to 350°F (180°C)
Greased cookie sheet

1. In a bowl, proof yeast according to package instructions.

2. In another bowl, mix together flour, sugar and salt. Using two knives, a pastry blender or your fingers, cut in butter and margarine until mixture resembles coarse crumbs. Make a well in the center. Add eggs, sour cream and dissolved yeast and mix well. Cover and refrigerate overnight.

3. Divide dough into four parts. Knead one part until soft, then on a work surface sprinkled with sugar-cinnamon mix, roll into a large circle, turning at least once so both sides will be coated with the sugar-cinnamon mixture. Using a knife or a pastry cutter, fluted if desired, cut into eight pie-shaped wedges and spread with sugar-cinnamon mix. Beginning with the outer edge and finishing with the point in the center roll up. Turn ends slightly towards each other to form a crescent. Repeat with remaining dough.

4. Place crescents 2 inches (5 cm) apart on prepared cookie sheet, cover with a clean tea towel and set in a warm place to rise until double in size, approximately 1 hour. Bake in preheated oven for 20 minutes until golden brown. Immediately transfer to wire racks to cool.

Makes 32 kiffles

Felicia's Mandelbrot

Mandelbrot, like Komish Bread, is a traditional Jewish cookie that is baked and sliced, then returned to the oven to dry. It is distinguished by the fact that it always contains almonds and, although it is similar to biscotti, it is not as hard.

2³/₄ cups	all-purpose flour	675 mL
4 tsp	baking powder	20 mL
¹/₂ tsp	salt	2 mL
3	eggs	3
1 cup	granulated sugar	250 mL
6 tbsp	vegetable oil	90 mL
	Grated zest of 1 lemon	
¹/₂ tsp	vanilla	2 mL
¹/₃ cup	coarsely chopped, blanched almonds	75 mL

Preheat oven to 350°F (180°C)
Lightly greased cookie sheet

1. In a bowl, sift together flour, baking powder and salt.

2. In another bowl, beat eggs, sugar, oil, zest and vanilla until thoroughly blended. Stir egg mixture into flour mixture and mix well. Fold in almonds and mix until a soft dough forms.

3. On a well-floured surface, divide dough in half. Shape into two long rolls about 3 inches (7.5 cm) wide. Place at least 2 inches (5 cm) apart on prepared sheet. Bake in preheated oven for 40 to 50 minutes until lightly browned and a toothpick inserted into center of one of the rolls comes out clean and dry. Remove from oven and turn off heat.

4. On a cutting board, cut hot rolls into slices about ¹/₂ inch (1 cm) thick. Place on cookie sheet and, leaving heat off, return to oven to dry for 25 minutes.

Makes about 3 dozen

Helen's Mon Cookies

Mon cookies are a traditional Jewish cookie made from poppy seeds.

1¹/₂ to 2 cups	all-purpose flour	375 to 500 mL
1 tsp	baking powder	5 mL
1 cup	old-fashioned rolled oats	250 mL
¹/₂ cup	softened shortening	125 mL
¹/₄ to ¹/₂ cup	vegetable oil	50 to 125 mL
³/₄ cup	packed brown sugar	175 mL
1	egg	1
¹/₄ cup	poppy seeds	50 mL

Preheat oven to 350°F (180°C)
Ungreased cookie sheet

1. In a bowl, mix together flour, baking powder and rolled oats.

2. In another bowl, cream together shortening, oil and brown sugar. Mix in egg and poppy seeds until well blended. Add flour mixture and mix well.

3. Drop by rounded teaspoonfuls (5 mL), about 2 inches (5 cm) apart, onto cookie sheet. Flatten slightly with a fork. Bake in preheated oven for 10 minutes until golden brown.

Makes about 3 dozen

Baba Mary's Thimble Cookies

1 cup	softened butter	250 mL
1/2 cup	lightly packed brown sugar	125 mL
2	egg yolks, beaten	2
2 cups	all-purpose flour	500 mL
2	egg whites, beaten	2
1 cup	chopped walnuts	250 mL
	Jam or jelly	

HINT: Rinse hot cookie sheet under cold water to cool completely before baking any more cookies.

Preheat oven to 300°F (150°C)
Ungreased cookie sheet

1. In a bowl, beat butter and brown sugar until smooth and creamy. Beat in egg yolks until well incorporated. Gradually add flour and mix until well blended.

2. Shape dough into 1-inch (2.5-cm) balls. Drop balls into slightly beaten egg whites and then into walnuts. Place about 1-inch (2.5-cm) apart on cookie sheet and, using a fork, flatten slightly. Using a thimble or your thumb, make an indentation in the center of each cookie and fill with jam or jelly. Bake in preheated oven for 15 to 20 minutes until golden brown. Immediately transfer to wire racks to cool.

Makes about 4 dozen

Colleen's Goosnargh Cakes

This recipe from a dear friend is for Goosnargh cakes, a barely sweetened shortbread with caraway seeds, which are a specialty of the northwest part of England.

1 tbsp	coriander seeds	15 mL
1 tbsp	caraway seeds	15 mL
1 lb	softened butter	500 g
1/4 cup	confectioner's (icing) sugar, sifted	50 mL
3 3/4 cups	all-purpose flour	925 mL
	Confectioner's (icing) sugar, sifted	

Preheat oven to 300°F (150°C)
Ungreased cookie sheet

1. Place seeds in a plastic bag and using a rolling pin, crush finely.

2. In a bowl, beat butter and confectioner's sugar until smooth and creamy. Add seeds and mix well. Gradually add flour, mixing well after each addition. (You may not need all the flour because dough should be moist, not dry.)

3. On a floured work surface, roll dough out to 3/4-inch (2-cm) thickness. Using a small glass, about 2 inch (5 cm) in diameter, cut out cookies. Place 2 inches (5 cm) apart on cookie sheet and bake in preheated oven for 30 to 45 minutes until just dry. Do not brown. Cookies should be white. Immediately transfer to wire racks to cool. When cool, sprinkle liberally with confectioner's sugar and pat to press down.

Makes 40 cookies

Aunty Giza's Rosettes

Aunty Giza always made her rosettes with glazed cherries, a variation I much prefer to the one made with jam.

1 cup	all-purpose flour	250 mL
1 tbsp	granulated sugar	15 mL
1/4 tsp	salt	1 mL
4	egg yolks, beaten	4
1	whole egg, beaten	1
1 tsp	lemon juice	5 mL
	Oil for frying	
	Confectioner's (icing) sugar, sifted	
	Glazed cherries, each cut into three or four pieces, or red jam or jelly	

HINT: For the smallest cookie cutter, use the top from a narrow-mouthed bottle such as ketchup.

HINT: When a recipe calls for just a few drops of lemon juice, poke holes in an uncut lemon with a fork and squeeze out the required amount. The lemon can go back into the refrigerator and be used several more times.

Round cookie cutters, 2 inches (5 cm), 1 inch (2.5 cm) and 1/2 inch (1 cm) in diameter
Deep fryer or Dutch oven

1. In a large bowl, mix together flour, sugar and salt. Make a well in the center. Add egg yolks, egg and lemon juice and mix until well blended.

2. On a floured surface, roll dough out to 1/8-inch (0.25-cm) thickness and, using the three cutters, make as many complete sets of different-sized circles as possible. Slit the edge of each round in five places to make petals. Combine three different-sized circles by placing the largest on the bottom and the smallest on the top. Using your finger, press hard in the center to stick layers together.

3. In a deep fryer or Dutch oven, heat oil to 375°F (190°C). Working with four to six rosettes at a time, fry cookies, turning once, to a golden brown. Using a slotted spoon lift out carefully and drain on paper towel. While still warm, dust with confectioner's sugar. Place a piece of glazed cherry or 1/4 tsp (1 mL) red jam or jelly in the center of each rosette.

Makes about 2 dozen

Shauna's Bow Knots

2	eggs	2
3 tbsp	granulated sugar	45 mL
1 tbsp	sour cream	15 mL
1/2 tsp	brandy	2 mL
1/2 tsp	any flavor liqueur	2 mL
1 3/4 cups	all-purpose flour, divided	425 mL
10 cups	vegetable oil for deep frying	2.5 L
	Confectioner's (icing) sugar, sifted	

Deep fryer or Dutch oven

1. In a bowl, beat eggs and sugar until light and fluffy. Add sour cream, brandy and liqueur, mixing until well blended. Gradually add 1 1/3 cups flour, in three portions, beating after each addition.

2. On a floured surface, knead in as much of remaining flour as required so dough is not sticky. Cover with a clean tea towel and let rest for 20 to 25 minutes.

3. Divide dough into four rolls. Place three pieces under a damp towel and roll one piece into a rectangle about 1/4 inch (0.5 cm) thick. Using a knife, cut into strips, 1x4 inches (2.5x10 cm). Cut a slit almost through the middle of the long side of the strip and take the two ends of each strip and pull them through the slit. Repeat with remaining dough.

4. Fill a deep fryer or Dutch oven with oil to a depth of about 2 inches (5 cm). Heat to 375°F (190°C). Add bows, a few at a time, and fry just until light golden brown (this will only take a few seconds). Lift out with a slotted spoon and drain on paper towel. Dust heavily with confectioner's sugar.

Makes about 3 dozen

Olga's Hamantashen

Prune Filling

1 cup	prunes, stones removed	250 mL
1 cup	raisins	250 mL
	Juice of 1 lemon	
	Juice of 1 orange	
1/2 cup	granulated sugar	125 mL
2 tsp	vanilla	10 mL
3 tbsp	apricot jam or other jam	45 mL
1 cup	finely crushed walnuts	250 mL

Dough

2/3 cup	softened shortening	160 mL
1 tsp	salt	5 mL
3 tbsp	liquid honey	45 mL
3	eggs	3
1 tsp	baking powder	5 mL
3 cups	all-purpose flour	750 mL

Topping

1	egg	1
2 tbsp	milk	25 mL
Pinch	sugar	Pinch

Preheat oven to 350°F (180°C)
Cookie cutter or glass 2 to 3 inches (5 to 7.5 cm) in diameter
Lightly greased cookie sheet

1. To make Prune Filling: In a bowl, cover prunes and raisins with boiling water and leave to soak overnight until softened. Drain.

2. In a food processor or using a mincer, process prunes and raisins until smooth. Transfer to a small bowl. Add lemon juice, orange juice, sugar, vanilla, jam and walnuts and mix well. Set aside.

3. In a bowl, cream shortening, salt and honey until smooth. Beat in eggs, one at a time, mixing until well incorporated. Stir in baking powder, then gradually add flour, mixing until a soft dough forms. Cover with a damp towel.

4. On a lightly floured surface, divide dough in half. Return one half to bowl and cover. Roll other half out to a 1/4-inch (0.5-cm) thickness. Using a cookie cutter dipped in flour, cut out circles. Spoon a heaping teaspoonful (5 cm) of filling in the center of each circle. Moisten the edges lightly with a finger dipped in water and pinch together three edges of the dough to form a triangle leaving a small opening in the center with some filling showing. It will resemble a three-cornered hat.

5. To make Topping: In a small bowl, beat the egg, milk and sugar. Brush on top of each triangle with the mixture.

6. Place triangles on prepared cookie sheet and bake in preheated oven for 15 to 20 minutes until nicely browned. Cool on sheet and using a spatula, lift off very carefully.

Makes about 2 dozen

Betty's Nothings

Nothing could be simpler than this very plain but delicious cookie.

3	eggs	3
3 tsp	granulated sugar	15 mL
Pinch	salt	Pinch
1/2 cup	vegetable oil	125 mL
1 cup	all-purpose flour	250 mL

Preheat oven to 425°F (220°C)
Greased cookie sheet

1. In a large bowl, beat eggs, sugar and salt until light and fluffy. Continue beating, gradually adding oil, alternately with flour. Mix well.

2. Drop by teaspoonfuls (5 mL), about 2 inches (5 cm) apart, onto prepared cookie sheet. Bake in preheated oven for 20 to 25 minutes or until lightly browned. Immediately transfer to wire racks to cool.

Makes about 3 dozen

Betty's Cornflake Macaroons

2	egg whites	2
1/2 tsp	vanilla	2 mL
1 cup	brown or granulated sugar	250 mL
2 cups	crushed cornflakes	500 mL
1/2 cup	chopped nuts	125 mL
1 cup	shredded coconut	250 mL

HINT: When making recipes that require egg whites only, drop the yolks into a pan of boiling, salted water and hard-cook them for use in salads, sandwiches, etc.

Preheat oven to 350°F (180°C)
Well-greased cookie sheet

1. Beat egg whites and vanilla until soft peaks form. Gradually beat in sugar until stiff peaks form. Gently fold in cornflakes, nuts and coconut.

2. Drop by rounded teaspoonfuls (5 mL), about 2 inches (5 cm) apart, onto prepared cookie sheet. Bake in preheated oven for 15 to 20 minutes or until delicately browned. Immediately transfer to wire racks to cool.

Makes about 2 1/2 dozen

Holiday Cookies

Many people associate holiday memories with special foods. The Thanksgiving Turkey, Christmas Pudding, Hanukah Rugelach and special baked goods are, for many, cherished traditions of the holidays. But homemade cookies are more than a holiday treat. They also make an ideal present. Wrapped in pretty paper or presented in elegant tins, they are always appreciated. From Peppermint Candy Canes to Poppy Seed Hamantashen, I hope these recipes will enhance your holiday celebrations.

Bird's Nest Cookies

3 cups	all-purpose flour	750 mL
1 tsp	baking powder	5 mL
1 tsp	salt	5 mL
1 cup	softened shortening	250 mL
1 cup	lightly packed brown sugar	250 mL
2	eggs, separated	2
1 tsp	vanilla	5 mL
1/2 cup	milk	125 mL
1 1/4 cups	sweetened shredded coconut	300 mL
1/2 cup	apricot or raspberry jam	125 mL

Preheat oven to 350°F (180°C)
Ungreased cookie sheet

1. In a bowl, mix together flour, baking powder and salt.

2. In another bowl, beat shortening and sugar until smooth and creamy. Add egg yolks, one at a time, beating until incorporated. Stir in vanilla. Gradually add flour mixture, alternating with milk to form a dough. Shape into 1 1/2-inch (4-cm) balls.

3. In a bowl, whisk eggs whites. Spread coconut on a plate. One at a time, dip balls into egg whites. Shake off excess, then roll in coconut. Place about 2 inches (5 cm) apart on cookie sheet and, using a thimble or your thumb, make a small dent in the center of each. Fill with jam.

4. Bake in preheated oven for 12 to 15 minutes until lightly browned. Immediately transfer to wire racks to cool.

Makes about 40 cookies

Xmas Chocolate Log Cookies

1 1/3 cups	granulated sugar	325 mL
2 tbsp	all-purpose flour	25 mL
Pinch	cinnamon	Pinch
2 1/2 cups	ground almonds	625 mL
2	egg whites	2
4	squares (each 1 oz/28 g) semi-sweet chocolate, melted (see page 11)	4
	Granulated sugar	

Preheat oven to 425°F (220°C)
Ungreased cookie sheet

1. In a bowl, mix together sugar, flour, cinnamon and almonds.

2. In another bowl, beat egg whites until soft peaks form. Fold in melted chocolate. Gradually add sugar mixture, mixing until a stiff dough forms.

3. On a lightly floured surface, shape dough, 2 tbsp (25 mL) at a time, into logs about 5 inches (12.5 cm) long, then roll in sugar. Place logs about 2 inches (5 cm) apart on cookie sheet. Bake in preheated oven for 10 minutes until browned. Using a lifter, carefully transfer to wire racks to cool.

Makes 4 dozen

Holiday Cranberry Cookies

1¹/₂ cups	all-purpose flour	375 mL
³/₄ tsp	baking powder	4 mL
¹/₄ tsp	baking soda	1 mL
¹/₄ tsp	salt	1 mL
¹/₄ cup	softened butter (¹/₂ stick)	50 mL
¹/₃ cup	packed brown sugar	75 mL
¹/₂ cup	granulated sugar	125 mL
1	egg	1
3 tbsp	orange juice concentrate	45 mL
1 tsp	grated orange zest	5 mL
1¹/₂ cups	fresh cranberries, halved or 1 cup (250 mL) dried cranberries	375 mL
¹/₂ cup	chopped pecans or walnuts	125 mL

Frosting

¹/₄ cup	softened butter	50 mL
2 cups	confectioner's (icing) sugar, sifted	500 mL
3 tbsp	frozen orange juice concentrate, thawed	45 mL
1 tsp	vanilla	5 mL
	Pecan or walnut halves (optional)	

Preheat oven to 375°F (190°C)
Ungreased cookie sheet

1. In a bowl, mix together flour, baking powder, baking soda and salt.

2. In another bowl, beat butter and sugars until smooth and creamy. Beat in egg until well incorporated. Stir in concentrate and zest until blended. Gradually add flour mixture and mix until well blended. Fold in cranberries and nuts until thoroughly combined.

3. Drop dough by rounded tablespoonfuls (15 mL), about 2 inches (5 cm) apart, onto cookie sheet. Bake in preheated oven for 10 to 12 minutes until lightly browned. Cool on cookie sheet.

4. To make Frosting: In a small bowl, beat butter until creamy. Add confectioner's sugar, orange juice and vanilla and mix until smooth. Spread on cooled cookies. Garnish with nuts, if desired.

Makes about 3 dozen

HINT: To prevent a crust from forming on icings and frostings, press a piece of plastic wrap against their surfaces until ready to use. If the plastic wrap won't cling to the bowl, moisten the rim before wrapping it. The plastic wrap will stick until you remove it.

Glazed Holiday Wreaths

1¼ cups	all-purpose flour	300 mL
½ cup	confectioner's (icing) sugar, sifted	125 mL
Pinch	salt	Pinch
½ cup	softened butter	125 mL
½ tsp	vanilla	2 mL
1	egg	1
Glaze		
1	egg, beaten	1
¼ cup	finely chopped blanched almonds	50 mL
2 tbsp	granulated sugar	25 mL

Preheat oven to 350°F (180°C)
Round cookie cutters or two glasses, 2½ inches (6 cm) and 1 inch (2.5 cm) in diameter
Ungreased cookie sheet

1. In a bowl, sift together flour, confectioner's sugar and salt.

2. In another bowl, beat butter, vanilla and egg until smooth and creamy. Add flour mixture and using your hands, knead into a dough.

3. Stir flour mixture into creamed mixture and using your hands knead into a dough. Divide dough into three portions. Wrap each tightly in plastic wrap and refrigerate for 1 to 2 hours until firm.

4. On a lightly floured surface, roll out dough to ⅛-inch (0.25-cm) thickness. Cut out circles with wide cutter, then using the smaller cutter, cut a circle in the center of each round. Place about 2 inches (5 cm) apart on cookie sheet. Brush with beaten egg, then top with almonds and sugar.

5. Bake in preheated oven for 10 to 15 minutes until golden brown. Cool on baking sheets for 5 minutes, then transfer to wire racks to cool completely.

Makes about 2½ dozen

Cherry Bell Cookies

³/₄ cup	softened butter (1¹/₂ sticks)	175 mL
¹/₂ cup	granulated sugar	125 mL
1	egg yolk	1
1 tsp	vanilla	5 mL
1³/₄ cups	all-purpose flour	425 mL
12	halved maraschino cherries, drained	12

HINT: Make extra dough when making cookies. Roll out and cut, shape and slice, then wrap tightly in plastic wrap and freeze. Unwrap and pop frozen dough into the oven whenever you want warm cookies in a hurry.

Preheat oven to 375°F (190°C)
Ungreased cookie sheet

1. In a bowl, beat butter and sugar until smooth and creamy. Beat in egg yolk and vanilla until well incorporated. Gradually beat in flour until a soft dough forms.

2. On a floured surface, roll dough into a log, 8x1¹/₂ inches (20x4 cm). Wrap tightly in plastic wrap and refrigerate at least 3 hours or overnight.

3. Using a knife, cut log into slices ¹/₄ inch (0.5 cm) wide and place about 2 inches (5 cm) apart on cookie sheet. Allow dough to reach room temperature, then fold two edges of each cookie over the center so they overlap with one end more pointed and the other a rounded bell shape. Tuck a cherry half into the rounded end to resemble a clapper. Bake in preheated oven 10 to 12 minutes until just lightly browned. Immediately transfer to wire racks to cool.

Makes about 2¹/₂ dozen

Chocolate Chunk Snowballs

2 cups	softened butter	500 mL
1 cup	confectioner's (icing) sugar, sifted	250 mL
3¹/₂ cups	all-purpose flour	875 mL
¹/₂ cup	cornstarch	125 mL
6	squares (each 1 oz/28 g) coarsely chopped bittersweet chocolate	6
1 cup	coarsely chopped pecans, toasted (see page 11)	250 mL
	Confectioner's (icing) sugar, sifted	

Preheat oven to 350°F (180°C)
Ungreased cookie sheet

1. In a bowl, beat butter and sugar until smooth and creamy. Gradually stir in flour, then cornstarch, mixing until well blended. Fold in chocolate and pecans.

2. Shape dough into 1-inch (2.5-cm) balls. Place about 2 inches (5 cm) apart on cookie sheet. Bake in preheated oven for 15 minutes until lightly browned. Immediately transfer to wire racks to cool. When cool, dust lightly with confectioner's sugar.

Makes about 5 dozen

Pfeffernüesse

These tasty cookies, traditionally served at Christmas in many European countries, are so-called because they contain an ingredient not usually found in cookies — black pepper.

4 cups	all-purpose flour	1 L
1 tsp	baking soda	5 mL
1/2 tsp	salt	2 mL
1/4 tsp	freshly ground black pepper	1 mL
1 tbsp	cinnamon	15 mL
1 tsp	nutmeg	5 mL
1 tsp	ground cloves	5 mL
1 tsp	allspice	5 mL
1 tbsp	ground cardamom seeds (optional)	15 mL
1/4 lb	candied orange peel	125 g
1/2 lb	citron (see Note, page 67)	250 g
2 tbsp	softened butter	25 mL
2 1/2 cups	confectioner's (icing) sugar, sifted	625 mL
5	eggs, separated	5
1 1/2 tsp	grated lemon zest	7 mL
	Confectioner's sugar for frosting (optional)	

Glaze (optional)

1 cup	confectioner's (icing) sugar	250 mL
1/4 cup	water	50 mL

HINT: Eggs separate easier when they are cold. However, egg whites will gain more volume if they are allowed to reach room temperature before being beaten.

Preheat oven to 350°F (180°C)
Ungreased cookie sheet

1. In a bowl, mix together flour, baking soda, salt, pepper, cinnamon, nutmeg, cloves, allspice, cardamom seeds, if using, orange peel and citron.

2. In another bowl, beat butter and confectioner's sugar until smooth and creamy. Beat in egg yolks and lemon zest until well blended. Add flour mixture and mix well.

3. In another bowl, beat egg whites until peaks form. Fold into flour-butter mixture. Wrap dough tightly in plastic wrap and refrigerate for 2 hours until firm.

4. Shape dough into 1-inch (2.5-cm) balls and place about 2 inches (5 cm) apart on cookie sheet. Bake in preheated oven for 15 minutes or until lightly browned.

5. To make Glaze: In a bowl, beat confectioner's sugar with water until smooth and spreadable. Spread lightly over tops of cookies and return to hot oven for 2 minutes. Immediately transfer to wire racks to cool.

Makes about 6 dozen

Rum-Glazed Xmas Fruitcake Cookies

1/2 cup + 2 tbsp	softened butter, divided	125 mL + 25 mL
1/3 cup	packed brown sugar	75 mL
1/2 tsp	cinnamon	2 mL
1/4 tsp	nutmeg	1 mL
1/2 tsp	ginger	2 mL
Pinch	salt	Pinch
1 cup + 2 tbsp	all-purpose flour, divided	250 mL + 25 mL
1/2 cup	moist dried figs, cut into 1/2-inch (1-cm) pieces	125 mL
1/2 cup	large dates, cut into 1/2-inch (1-cm) pieces	125 mL
1/2 cup	blanched almonds, toasted and chopped (see page 11)	125 mL
1/2 cup	coarsely chopped pecans	125 mL
2 tbsp	liquid honey	25 mL
1 tsp	rum	5 mL
1	egg, lightly beaten	1

Rum Glaze

1/2 cup	confectioner's (icing) sugar, sifted	125 mL
2 tbsp	dark rum	25 mL

NOTE: Just like Christmas fruitcake, these cookies will be better if they are allowed to mellow for 2 to 3 days after they are baked. Store in an airtight container for up to 2 weeks.

Preheat oven to 400°F (200°C)
2-inch (5-cm) round cookie cutter, fluted if possible
Lightly greased cookie sheet

1. In a bowl, beat 6 tbsp (90 mL) butter and brown sugar until smooth and creamy. Add cinnamon, nutmeg, ginger and salt and beat until well combined. Add 3/4 cup (175 mL) flour and mix until a soft dough forms. Wrap tightly in plastic wrap and refrigerate for 15 to 30 minutes until firm.

2. In another bowl, mix together figs, dates, almonds and pecans.

3. In a clean bowl, beat remaining butter, honey and rum until smooth and creamy. Gradually beat in egg until incorporated. Add remaining flour and mix well. Add to fruit mixture, mixing until pieces are completely coated. Set aside.

4. On a lightly floured surface, roll dough out to 1/4-inch (0.5-cm) thickness. Using a cookie cutter dipped in flour, cut out rounds and place 2 inches (5 cm) apart on prepared cookie sheet. Drop a rounded tablespoonful (15 mL) of the fruit and nut mixture onto each cookie and using your fingers, shape into mounds. Bake in preheated oven for 10 to 12 minutes until cookies begin to brown on the top.

5. To make Rum Glaze: In a bowl, beat confectioner's sugar and rum until smooth. Spread over hot cookies and immediately return to preheated oven to bake for 1 minute until glaze bubbles. Cool on cookie sheet for 5 minutes, then transfer to wire racks to cool completely.

Makes about 2 dozen

Springerle Cookies

Springerle are German cookies, usually made at Christmas. They are noted for their beautiful designs, achieved by using either a special rolling pin or individual molds.

4 cups	all-purpose flour	1 L
1 tsp	baking soda	5 mL
4	eggs	4
2 cups	granulated sugar	500 mL
2 tsp	anise extract	10 mL
2 tbsp	crushed anise seeds	25 mL

NOTE: An egg left at room temperature for one hour deteriorates as much as it would if stored for a week in the refrigerator. Eggs should be stored in their carton, in the refrigerator, not on the refrigerator door.

Preheat oven to 300°F (150°C)
Springerle rolling pin or molds
Lightly floured cookie sheets
Greased cookie sheets
Airtight container

1. In a bowl, mix together flour and baking soda.

2. In another bowl, beat eggs and sugar until smooth and creamy. Stir in anise extract. Stir in flour, one-third at a time, mixing after each addition, until a stiff dough forms.

3. Divide dough into three portions. On a lightly floured surface, using a plain rolling pin, roll dough out to $1/2$-inch (1-cm) thickness. Flour the springerle rolling pin, if using, and roll slowly, only once, over the dough, pressing down firmly to make clear designs. Your cookies will now be about $1/4$ inch (0.5 cm) thick. Cut cookies apart on dividing lines. Lift each cookie carefully and transfer to lightly floured cookie sheets. Repeat with remaining dough. Cover with towels and let stand overnight. If using springerle molds, roll the dough a bit thinner with the plain rolling pin and press molds firmly into the dough. Then transfer to floured sheets.

4. Grease a clean cookie sheet and sprinkle lightly with anise seeds. Brush excess flour from cookie bottoms and using a finger dipped in water, moisten bottom of each cookie. Place about 2 inches (5 cm) apart on prepared cookie sheet. Bake in preheated oven for 15 minutes until firm and dry, but not browned. Immediately transfer to wire racks to cool. Allow cookies to mellow in a covered, airtight container for at least 1 week.

Makes about 6 dozen

Peppermint Candy Canes

2½ cups	all-purpose flour	625 mL
1 tsp	salt	5 mL
½ cup	softened shortening	125 mL
½ cup	softened butter or margarine	125 mL
1 cup	confectioner's (icing) sugar, sifted	250 mL
1	egg	1
1 tsp	vanilla	5 mL
1 tsp	peppermint extract	5 mL
½ tsp or more	red food coloring	2 mL or more

Preheat oven to 375°F (190°C)
Ungreased cookie sheet

1. In a bowl, mix together flour and salt.

2. In another bowl, beat shortening, butter or margarine and confectioner's sugar until smooth. Beat in egg until well incorporated. Stir in vanilla and peppermint extract and mix well. Gradually add flour mixture and mix until a dough forms.

3. On a lightly floured surface, divide dough into two portions. Knead red food coloring into one portion until well blended. Leave other portion as is.

4. Shape 1 tsp (5 mL) of dough from each half into a 4-inch (10-cm) long rope, roll back and forth until smooth and even. Place plain rope and a red colored one side by side. Twist together to make a candy cane. Repeat with remaining dough.

5. Place canes on cookie sheet and using your hand, curve the top of each to form the handle of a cane. Bake in preheated oven for 8 to 10 minutes until firm and lightly browned. Immediately transfer to wire racks to cool.

Makes about 4 dozen

Christmas Fruit Cookies

4 cups	all-purpose flour	1 L
2 tsp	baking powder	10 mL
1/2 tsp	salt	2 mL
3/4 cup	softened butter or margarine	175 mL
3/4 cup	softened shortening	175 mL
1 1/4 cups	packed brown sugar	300 mL
2	eggs	2
1 tsp	vanilla	5 mL
1	can (8 oz/250 mL) crushed pineapple, drained	1
1/2 cup	chopped red maraschino cherries	125 mL
1/2 cup	chopped green maraschino cherries	125 mL
1/2 cup	chopped dates	125 mL
1/2 cup	chopped pecans or walnuts	125 mL
1/2 cup	shredded coconut (optional)	125 mL

Preheat oven to 375°F (190°C)
Ungreased cookie sheet

1. In a bowl, mix together flour, baking powder and salt.

2. In another bowl, beat butter or margarine, shortening and brown sugar until smooth and creamy. Beat in eggs, one at a time, until incorporated. Stir in vanilla. Gradually add flour mixture, mixing until well combined. Stir in pineapple, red and green cherries, dates, nuts and coconut, if desired. Mix well until thoroughly combined.

3. On a lightly floured surface, divide dough into three portions. Shape each portion into a roll 10 inches (25 cm) long. Wrap each roll tightly in plastic wrap and refrigerate for 2 hours until firm.

4. On a cutting board, cut dough into slices 1/4 inch (0.5 cm) thick. Place about 2 inches (5 cm) apart on cookie sheets. Bake in preheated oven for 8 to 10 minutes until golden brown. Immediately transfer to wire racks to cool.

Makes about 10 dozen

Chocolate Thumbprint Cookies

2 cups	all-purpose flour	500 mL
1/4 cup	cocoa	50 mL
1 cup	softened butter	250 mL
1/2 cup	granulated sugar	125 mL
2	eggs	2
1 tsp	vanilla	5 mL
1 cup	finely chopped pecans	250 mL
18	halved glazed cherries	18
	Melted semi-sweet or bittersweet chocolate (see page 11) (optional)	

Preheat oven to 325°F (160°C)
Greased cookie sheet

1. In a bowl, mix together flour and cocoa.

2. In another bowl, beat butter and sugar until smooth and creamy. Beat in eggs, one at a time, until incorporated. Stir in vanilla. Gradually add flour mixture, mixing until well incorporated. Fold in pecans.

3. Shape dough into 1-inch (2.5-cm) balls and press a cherry halve into the center. Place about 2 inches (5 cm) apart on prepared cookie sheet. Bake in preheated oven for 15 minutes until golden brown. Immediately transfer to wire racks to cool. When cool, drizzle melted chocolate over tops in a zigzag pattern, if desired.

Makes about 3 dozen

Mincemeat Drop Cookies

1 1/2 cups	all-purpose flour	375 mL
1 1/2 tsp	baking soda	7 mL
1/2 tsp	cinnamon	2 mL
1/4 tsp	nutmeg	1 mL
1/4 tsp	salt	1 mL
1/4 cup	softened butter or margarine	50 mL
3/4 cup	packed brown sugar	175 mL
2	eggs	2
3/4 cup	mincemeat	175 mL
1 1/2 cups	semi-sweet chocolate chips	375 mL
1/2 cup	chopped walnuts	125 mL

Preheat oven to 350°F (180°C)
Greased cookie sheet

1. In a bowl, mix together flour, baking soda, cinnamon, nutmeg and salt.

2. In another bowl, beat butter or margarine and brown sugar until smooth and creamy. Add eggs, one at a time, beating until well incorporated. Stir in mincemeat. Add flour mixture and mix until thoroughly combined. Fold in chocolate chips and nuts.

3. Drop by tablespoonfuls (15 mL), about 2 inches (5 cm) apart, onto prepared cookie sheet. Bake in preheated oven for 10 to 12 minutes until golden brown. Immediately transfer to wire racks to cool.

Makes about 4 dozen

Checkerboard Squares

1 cup	softened butter or margarine (2 sticks)	250 mL
½ cup	granulated sugar	125 mL
6 tbsp	packed brown sugar	90 mL
1	egg	1
2 tsp	vanilla	10 mL
1½ tsp	baking powder	7 mL
1½ cups + 2 tbsp	all-purpose flour	375 mL + 25 mL
2	squares (each 1 oz/28 g) unsweetened chocolate, melted (see page 11)	2

Preheat oven to 375°F (190°C)
Ungreased cookie sheet

1. In a bowl, beat butter or margarine and sugars until smooth and creamy. Beat in egg until incorporated. Stir in vanilla and baking powder.

2. Gradually add flour, mixing in as much as possible, then stirring in remainder with a wooden spoon.

3. Divide dough in half. Knead melted chocolate into one portion of dough until combined. Divide plain and chocolate doughs in half. Shape each portion into 8-inch (20-cm) logs. (You will have two plain logs and two chocolate logs.) Wrap each tightly in plastic wrap and refrigerate for 2 hours until firm.

4. On a floured surface, place one plain roll and one chocolate roll side by side. Top the plain roll with another chocolate roll and the chocolate roll with a plain roll. Press logs together firmly so they adhere and, using your hands, square the sides to make a square-shaped log. Wrap tightly in plastic wrap and refrigerate 6 hours until firm.

5. Using a knife, cut log into slices ¼ inch (0.5 cm) thick. Place about 2 inches (5 cm) apart on cookie sheet. Bake in preheated oven for 8 to 10 minutes until bottoms are lightly browned. Immediately transfer to wire racks to cool.

Makes about 6 dozen

Double Chocolate Swirl Cookies

1 tbsp	hot water (not boiling)	15 mL
1½ tsp	instant coffee (espresso) granules	7 mL
2¼ cups	all-purpose flour	550 mL
¼ cup	unsweetened cocoa	50 mL
1 cup	softened butter or margarine	250 mL
⅓ cup	firmly packed brown sugar	75 mL
⅓ cup	granulated sugar	75 mL
1	egg	1
1 tsp	vanilla	5 mL
2	squares (each 1 oz/28 g) semi-sweet chocolate, melted and cooled (see page 11)	2

Chocolate Dip

3	squares (each 1 oz/28 g) white chocolate, melted	3
3	squares (each 1 oz/28 g) semi-sweet chocolate, melted	3

> **HINT:** Before pouring hot liquid into a glass, place a stainless steel spoon in the glass. Add the liquid slowly so the spoon can absorb the heat and the glass won't crack.

Preheat oven to 375°F (190°C)
Pastry bag with star tip
Lightly greased cookie sheet
Large platter or cookie sheet lined with waxed paper

1. In a cup, mix hot water and coffee granules until coffee dissolves. Set aside to cool.

2. In a bowl, mix together flour and cocoa.

3. In another bowl, beat butter or margarine and sugars until smooth and creamy. Beat in egg until incorporated. Stir in vanilla and melted chocolate until blended. Add coffee and mix well. Gradually add flour mixture, beating until just blended.

4. Using a pastry bag with a star tip, pipe dough onto prepared cookie sheet, making a 2-inch (5-cm) circle with a swirled design. Bake in preheated oven for 8 to 10 minutes until lightly browned. Immediately transfer to wire racks to cool.

5. Holding a cookie with your fingers, dip top half in white chocolate. Place on a platter or cookie sheet lined with waxed paper. Repeat with 13 additional cookies. Drizzle top of the dipped half with semi-sweet chocolate. Repeat procedure for remaining cookies, but dip in semi-sweet chocolate and drizzle with white chocolate.

Makes 2½ dozen

Chocolate Chip Holiday Stars

2¹/₂ cups	all-purpose flour	625 mL
¹/₂ tsp	salt	2 mL
1 cup	softened butter or margarine	250 mL
¹/₃ cup	granulated sugar	75 mL
¹/₂ cup	packed brown sugar	125 mL
1	egg yolk	1
2 tsp	vanilla	10 mL
2 cups	mini semi-sweet chocolate chips, divided	500 mL
	Vanilla Icing (see Recipe, page 37)	

HINT: If you are baking cookie dough containing chocolate bits, flouring a greased baking sheet will prevent the chocolate from sticking and burning if it comes in direct contact with the baking sheet.

HINT: To decorate cookies with frosting when you don't have a decorator, cut an envelope from one of the top corners to the middle of the bottom of the envelope. Cut a little piece off the corner. Fill with some frosting and squeeze out as you would with a decorator.

Preheat oven to 350°F (180°C)
Ungreased cookie sheets
Star-shaped cookie cutter
Cake decorating tube with a fine tip

1. In a bowl, mix together flour and salt.

2. In another bowl, beat butter or margarine and sugars until smooth and creamy. Add egg yolk and beat until incorporated. Stir in vanilla. Gradually add flour mixture, mixing until a soft dough forms. Stir in 1¹/₂ cups (375 mL) chocolate chips.

3. Divide dough in half. Flatten each half into a disk and wrap tightly in plastic wrap. Cover and refrigerate for 1 to 2 hours until firm.

4. Place one portion of dough between two sheets of waxed paper and roll out to ¹/₄-inch (0.5-cm) thickness. Using a star cookie cutter, cut into star shapes and place about 2 inches (5 cm) apart on cookie sheets. Cover with clean towel and refrigerate for 10 minutes. Bake in preheated oven for 10 to 12 minutes until golden brown. Cool 5 minutes on sheet then transfer to wire racks to cool completely.

5. Melt remaining ¹/₂ cup (125 mL) chocolate chips (see page 11). Using a cake decorator tube with a fine, straight-line tip, pipe a thin line of chocolate close to outer edge of cookie following the shape of the star. Repeat with vanilla icing, drawing a second line inside the chocolate outline.

Makes about 3 dozen

Raspberry Bows

2¼ cups	all-purpose flour, divided	550 mL
1	package (¼ oz/8 g) quick-rising active dry yeast	1
½ cup	sour cream	125 mL
1 tbsp	water	15 mL
½ cup	softened butter	125 mL
1	egg	1
	Granulated sugar	

Raspberry Filling

2 tbsp	softened butter	25 mL
⅓ cup	raspberry jam	75 mL
¼ cup	plain bread crumbs	50 mL
¼ cup	granulated sugar	50 mL
	Confectioner's (icing) sugar, sifted	

HINT: If something spills in your oven while baking, immediately sprinkle salt over the spill. Once the oven has cooled, brush off the burnt food and wipe clean with a damp sponge.

Preheat oven to 375°F (190°C)
Cookie sheet lined with parchment or waxed paper

1. In a bowl, combine ½ cup (125 mL) flour with the yeast.

2. In a small saucepan, heat sour cream with water until warm (not hot). Stir into flour mixture. Add butter, egg and as much of the remaining flour as necessary to make a soft dough.

3. Knead dough into a ball. Divide in half and wrap each half tightly in plastic wrap. Refrigerate for 2 to 3 hours.

4. To make Raspberry Filling: In a small bowl, mix together butter, jam, bread crumbs and sugar. Set aside.

5. On a work surface, sprinkled with granulated sugar, roll one portion of dough into an 18x8-inch (45x20-cm) rectangle. Spread half of the filling, lengthwise, over half of the dough. Fold dough in half, lengthwise, and trim the edges. Cut crosswise into 12 strips and twist each in the center to form a bow. Repeat with remaining dough.

6. Place bows about 2 inches (5 cm) apart on prepared cookie sheet. Bake in preheated oven for 15 to 20 minutes until golden brown. Immediately transfer to wire racks. When cool, dust with sifted confectioner's sugar.

Makes 2 dozen

Hickory Nut Macaroons

2	egg whites	2
2 cups	confectioner's (icing) sugar, sifted	500 mL
1 cup	chopped hickory nuts or toasted pecans (see page 11)	250 mL

Preheat oven to 325°F (160°C)
Greased cookie sheet

1. In a bowl, beat egg whites until soft peaks form. Add confectioner's sugar, $1/4$ cup (50 mL) at a time, beating until stiff peaks form. Fold in nuts.

2. Drop by rounded teaspoonfuls (5 mL), about 2 inches (5 cm) apart, onto prepared cookie sheet. Bake in preheated oven for 15 minutes until edges are lightly browned. (Cookies may split around the edges as they bake, which is acceptable.) Immediately transfer to wire racks to cool. Recipe can be doubled.

Makes about 1 1/2 dozen

Hanukah Sugar Cookies

2 cups	all-purpose flour	500 mL
$1^1/_2$ tsp	baking powder	7 mL
$^1/_2$ tsp	salt	2 mL
$^1/_4$ tsp	nutmeg	1 mL
$^3/_4$ cup	softened butter or margarine	175 mL
1 cup	granulated sugar	250 mL
2	eggs	2
1 tsp	vanilla	5 mL
	Vanilla Icing (see Recipe, page 37) (optional)	

Preheat oven to 375°F (190°C)
Ungreased cookie sheet
Cookie cutters in Hanukah shapes, such as a dreidel, menorah or Star of David

1. In a bowl, mix together flour, baking powder, salt and nutmeg.

2. In another bowl, beat butter or margarine and sugar until smooth and creamy. Beat in eggs, one at a time, until incorporated. Stir in vanilla. Gradually add flour mixture, mixing until a soft dough forms. Cover tightly and refrigerate for 2 to 3 hours until firm.

3. On a lightly floured surface, roll dough out to $1/8$-inch (0.25-cm) thickness. Using cookie cutters, cut into a variety of Hanukah shapes. Place 2 inches (5 cm) apart on cookie sheet. Bake in preheated oven for 8 to 10 minutes until lightly browned. Immediately transfer to wire racks to cool. Decorate cookies with icing, if desired.

Makes about 3 dozen

Cinnamon Nut Rugelach

1 cup	softened butter (2 sticks)	250 mL
1	package (8 oz/250 g) softened cream cheese	1
2	eggs	2
1 tsp	salt	5 mL
2¹/₂ cups	all-purpose flour	625 mL
Cinnamon–Nut Filling		
³/₄ cup	finely chopped raisins	175 mL
²/₃ cup	finely chopped walnuts	160 mL
1 cup	granulated sugar	250 mL
¹/₂ tsp	cinnamon	2 mL
¹/₂ cup	melted butter	125 mL

VARIATION

Chocolate-Coconut Filling

In a small bowl, mix together ¹/₂ cup (125 mL) finely chopped slivered toasted almonds, ³/₄ cup (175 mL) shredded, sweetened coconut, ¹/₂ cup (125 mL) semi-sweet mini chocolate chips and 4 tbsp (50 mL) granulated sugar. Using a spatula, thinly coat a large circle of dough with 2 tbsp (25 mL) apricot preserves. Sprinkle with a quarter of the almond mixture. Proceed with Step 5 right.

Preheat oven to 375°F (190°C)
Cookie sheet lined with parchment or waxed paper

1. In a bowl, beat butter and cream cheese until smooth. Add eggs, one at a time, beating until incorporated. Mix in salt, then gradually beat in flour, until a sticky dough forms. Transfer dough to a lightly floured surface and knead, adding up to ¹/₂ cup (125 mL) flour until dough is not sticky.

2. Divide dough into four portions. Wrap each in plastic wrap and refrigerate for 3 to 4 hours until firm.

3. To make Cinnamon-Nut Filling: In a small bowl, combine raisins and walnuts. Add sugar and cinnamon and mix well. Set aside.

4. On floured surface, roll one portion of dough into a 10-inch (25-cm) circle. Brush with melted butter and sprinkle about ¹/₃ cup (75 mL) nut mixture over the circle.

5. Using a knife or pastry cutter, cut circle into 12 pie-shaped wedges. Roll up tightly, beginning from the wide edge and finishing with the point in the middle. Bend the rolls slightly inward to form crescents and place, point side down, about 2 inches (5 cm) apart, on prepared cookie sheet. Brush with melted butter. Repeat with remaining dough.

6. Bake in preheated oven for 20 to 25 minutes until golden brown. Immediately transfer to wire racks to cool.

Makes about 4 dozen

Passover Almond Cookies

3	eggs	3
1/2 cup	granulated sugar	125 mL
1 tbsp	matzo meal	15 mL
2 tbsp	brandy	25 mL
2 1/4 cups	finely ground almonds or hazelnuts	550 mL
	Halved blanched almonds	

Preheat oven to 300°F (150°C)
Lightly greased cookie sheet

1. In a medium bowl, whisk eggs until light and fluffy. Add sugar and matzo meal and mix well. Stir in brandy. Fold in nuts until well combined.

2. Shape dough into 1-inch (2.5-cm) balls. Place about 2 inches (5 cm) apart on prepared cookie sheet and gently press half a nut in the center of each. Bake in preheated oven for 20 minutes until lightly browned. Immediately transfer to wire racks to cool.

Makes about 2 1/2 dozen

Passover Coconut Macaroons

2	egg whites	2
1/2 cup	granulated sugar	125 mL
1 tbsp	liquid honey	15 mL
2 tbsp	potato starch	25 mL
1 3/4 cups	finely shredded coconut (see Note, below)	425 mL

NOTE: This recipe works best if the coconut is very fine. Add required quantity to a food processor and process to the desired consistency.

Preheat oven to 325°F (160°C)
Greased cookie sheet dusted with potato starch

1. In a bowl, beat egg whites until soft peaks form. Add sugar and honey and beat until shiny, stiff peaks form. Gradually fold in potato starch, then coconut.

2. Drop by tablespoonfuls (15 mL), about 2 inches (5 cm) apart, onto prepared cookie sheet. Bake in preheated oven for 15 to 18 minutes until lightly browned. Immediately transfer to wire racks to cool.

Makes about 2 1/2 dozen

Poppy Seed Hamantashen

These cookies, which are made in the shape of a three-cornered hat, are traditionally made to celebrate the Jewish feast of Purim. (For prune filling, see Olga's Hamantashen, page 149.)

6	eggs	6
1 cup	vegetable oil	250 mL
1 cup	granulated sugar	250 mL
	Juice of $1/2$ lemon or $1/2$ cup (125 mL) orange juice	
6 cups	all-purpose flour	1.5 L
4 tsp	baking powder	20 mL
$1/4$ tsp	salt	1 mL
Poppy Seed Filling		
2 cups	poppy seeds	500 mL
$3/4$ cup	milk	175 mL
$1/2$ cup	liquid honey	125 mL
$1/4$ cup	brown sugar	50 mL
Pinch	salt	Pinch
1	egg, beaten	
Glaze		
1	egg yolk, lightly beaten	1

Preheat oven to 350°F (180°C)
3-inch (7.5-cm) round cookie cutter
Greased cookie sheet

1. In a bowl, whisk together eggs, oil, sugar and juice until blended.

2. In another bowl, sift together flour, baking powder and salt. Make a well in the center. Pour in egg mixture and using your hands, mix together until a soft dough forms. Cover and refrigerate for 2 hours or overnight.

3. To make Poppy Seed Filling: In a bowl, add boiling water to poppy seeds to cover by 1 inch (2.5 cm). Let stand for 10 minutes, then drain. In a food processor with a metal blade, grind poppy seeds.

4. In a saucepan, combine ground poppy seeds, milk, honey, brown sugar and salt. Cook over low heat for 5 minutes, stirring constantly, until thick. Allow to cool for 15 minutes, then mix in beaten egg. Set aside.

5. On a lightly floured surface, roll dough into a circle about $1/8$ inch (0.25 cm) thick. Using a 3-inch (7.5-cm) cookie cutter, cut out circles. Spoon a heaping tablespoonful (15 mL) of filling in the center of each circle. Moisten the edges lightly with a finger dipped in water and pinch together three edges of the dough to form a triangle leaving a small opening in the center with some filling showing. It will resemble a three-cornered hat. Or pinch the top together tightly to enclose the filling, if desired.

6. Place triangles on prepared cookie sheet. Cover with a cloth and let stand for 1 hour. Then brush tops with egg yolk glaze. Bake in preheated oven for 20 to 25 minutes until lightly browned. Allow to cool on sheets, then using a spatula, lift off very carefully.

Makes about $3^1/2$ dozen

Chocolate Valentine Hearts

1 cup	softened butter	250 mL
1 cup	confectioner's (icing) sugar, sifted	250 mL
1/3 cup	cocoa	75 mL
1 1/2 cups	all-purpose flour	375 mL
	Vanilla Icing (see Recipe, page 37)	
	Cinnamon hearts for decoration	

HINT: When using recipe cards, place a fork, tines up, in a tall glass and wedge the card between the tines.

Preheat oven to 300°F (150°C)
Ungreased cookie sheet
3-inch (7.5-cm) heart-shaped cookie cutter

1. In a large bowl, cream butter until smooth.

2. In another bowl, sift confectioner's sugar, cocoa and flour. Gradually add to butter and mix until a soft dough forms. If dough is too soft, refrigerate for 30 minutes until firm.

3. On a lightly floured surface, roll dough to 1/8-inch (0.25-cm) thickness. Using a heart-shaped cookie cutter, about 3 inches (7.5 cm) across, cut out cookies. Place about 2 inches (5 cm) apart on cookie sheet and bake in preheated oven for 20 to 25 minutes. Cool on sheet for 5 minutes, then transfer to wire racks to cool completely.

4. Make Vanilla Icing and divide in half. Tint one half with red food coloring. Decorate with red and white icing, cinnamon hearts, whatever strikes your fancy as appropriate for Valentine's Day.

Makes about 3 dozen

Cherry Valentine Cookies

3¹/₂ cups	all-purpose flour	825 mL
2 tsp	baking powder	10 mL
1 tsp	baking soda	5 mL
¹/₂ tsp	salt	2 mL
¹/₂ cup	softened shortening	125 mL
¹/₂ cup	softened butter or margarine	125 mL
1 cup	granulated sugar	250 mL
1	egg	1
1 tsp	vanilla	5 mL
¹/₂ cup	milk	125 mL

Cherry Filling

¹/₂ cup	granulated sugar	125 mL
4¹/₂ tsp	cornstarch	22 mL
¹/₂ cup	orange juice	125 mL
1 tbsp	butter or margarine	15 mL
12	red maraschino cherries, chopped	12
¹/₄ cup	cherry juice	50 mL
	Additional sugar	

NOTE: To use little hearts from leftover cut outs lower oven heat to 325°F (160°C) and bake 5 minutes until lightly browned. Dip in melted chocolate, if desired.

HINT: Dip cookie cutters in salad oil before cutting out cookies. It will make a cleaner cut and be less sticky.

Preheat oven to 375°F (190°C)
Greased cookie sheet
Large and small heart-shaped cookie cutters

1. In a bowl, mix together flour, baking powder, baking soda and salt.

2. In another bowl, beat shortening, butter or margarine and sugar until smooth and creamy. Add egg and beat until well incorporated. Stir in vanilla and milk until well blended. Gradually add flour mixture, mixing until a soft dough forms. Cover and refrigerate for at least 2 hours until firm.

3. To make Cherry Filling: In a small saucepan, combine sugar, cornstarch, orange juice, butter or margarine, cherries and cherry juice. Bring to a boil over low heat and cook, stirring, for 1 minute. Transfer saucepan to refrigerator and chill until cool.

4. On a lightly floured surface, roll dough out to ¹/₈-inch (0.25-cm) thickness. Using a heart-shaped cookie cutter, about 2¹/₂ inches (6 cm) across, cut cookies out. Place half on prepared cookie sheet. Spoon ¹/₂ tsp (2 mL) filling in the center of each. Using a heart-shaped cookie cutter, about 1¹/₂ inches (4 cm) across, cut hearts out of remaining cookies. Place cut-out hearts over filled hearts and press together gently.

5. Bake in preheated oven for 8 to 10 minutes until lightly browned. Immediately transfer to wire racks to cool.

Makes about 4¹/₂ dozen

Thanksgiving Pumpkin Spice Cookies

4 1/2 cups	all-purpose flour	1.125 L
2 tsp	baking powder	10 mL
1 tsp	baking soda	5 mL
1 1/2 tsp	cinnamon	7 mL
1/2 tsp	nutmeg	2 mL
1/2 tsp	ginger	2 mL
1 1/4 cups	softened shortening	300 mL
1 cup	packed brown sugar	250 mL
1 cup	granulated sugar	250 mL
2	eggs	2
1 tsp	vanilla	5 mL
1 tsp	finely grated orange zest	5 mL
1	can (16 oz) pumpkin purée	1
	Confectioner's (icing) sugar, sifted	

Preheat oven to 375°F (190°C)
Round cookie cutter or glass, 2 inches (5 cm) in diameter
Ungreased cookie sheet

1. In a bowl, mix together flour, baking powder, baking soda, cinnamon, nutmeg and ginger.

2. In another bowl, beat shortening and sugars until smooth and creamy. Beat in eggs, one at a time, until incorporated. Stir in vanilla and orange zest. Add half the flour mixture and beat well. Add pumpkin and beat well. Add remaining flour mixture, beating until well combined and a soft dough forms.

3. Divide dough in half. Wrap each portion tightly in plastic wrap and refrigerate for 3 to 4 hours until firm.

4. On a lightly floured surface, roll out one portion of dough to 1/4-inch (0.5-cm) thickness. Using a cutter dipped in flour, cut into rounds and place about 2 inches (5 cm) apart on cookie sheet. Bake in preheated oven for 10 minutes until browned. Immediately transfer to wire racks to cool. When cool, dust with sifted confectioner's sugar.

Makes about 6 dozen

Candied Easter Specials

2 cups	all-purpose flour	500 mL
1/4 tsp	baking soda	1 mL
Pinch	salt	Pinch
1/2 tsp	cinnamon	2 mL
1/4 tsp	nutmeg	1 mL
Pinch	ground cloves	Pinch
1 cup	liquid honey	250 mL
1 tbsp	granulated sugar	15 mL
1/4 cup	chopped blanched almonds	50 mL
2 tbsp	softened butter or margarine	25 mL
1 tbsp	rum or sherry	15 mL
3/4 tsp	grated lemon zest	4 mL
1/2 cup	chopped candied lemon or orange peel	125 mL
	Granulated sugar (optional)	

NOTE: These cookies are best stored in an airtight container with a slice of apple to keep them moist.

Preheat oven to 300°F (150°C)
Greased cookie sheet
Round or rectangular cookie cutter

1. In a bowl, sift together flour, baking soda, salt, cinnamon, nutmeg and cloves.

2. In a small saucepan, over low heat, bring honey and sugar to a boil, stirring constantly. Simmer for 5 minutes, then add almonds and simmer 5 minutes more. Set aside to cool.

3. In a bowl, beat butter or margarine, rum or sherry and lemon zest. Add honey mixture and blend well. Gradually add flour mixture and mix well. Stir in candied peel, mixing until a soft dough forms. Cover and refrigerate for 1 to 2 hours until firm.

4. On a lightly floured surface, divide dough into three portions. Roll one portion out to 1/4- to 1/2-inch (0.5- to 1-cm) thickness. Using a round or rectangular cookie cutter dipped in flour, cut out shapes. Repeat with remaining dough.

5. Place cookies about 2 inches (5 cm) apart on prepared cookie sheet. Bake in preheated oven for 20 minutes until browned. Immediately transfer to wire racks to cool. While cookies are still warm, sprinkle with granulated sugar, if desired.

Makes about 3 dozen

Chinese New Year Bursts

2 cups	all-purpose flour	500 mL
1 tsp	baking powder	5 mL
1 tbsp	softened shortening	15 mL
$^2/_3$ cup	granulated sugar	160 mL
1	egg	1
3 tbsp	water	45 mL
$^1/_2$ cup	sesame seeds	125 mL
8 cups	vegetable oil	2 L

NOTE: If you don't have a deep-frying thermometer, you can test the temperature of the oil by dropping a small piece of bread into it. If it turns golden in color, the oil is hot enough.

Deep fryer or Dutch oven
Preheat oil to 325°F (160°C)

1. In a small bowl, mix together flour and baking powder.

2. In a bowl, beat shortening and sugar until smooth and creamy. Beat in egg until well incorporated. Add water and mix until well blended. Stir in flour mixture, mixing until a dough forms.

3. On a lightly floured surface, knead dough until soft. Shape into $1^1/_2$-inch (4-cm) balls.

4. Add water to a bowl and spread sesame seeds on a plate. Dip balls in water, then roll in sesame seeds to coat.

5. Heat oil in deep fryer or Dutch oven. Using a slotted spoon, add five or six balls to heated oil. Cook, turning once, until dough cracks in the center, bursts and is golden brown, about 3 to 5 minutes. Using a slotted spoon, transfer cookies to a paper towel to drain. Repeat with remaining dough.

Makes about 16 bursts

Shortbread

Traditional Scottish shortbread is one of the best-known and best-loved cookies in the world. Served with tea, there are few more satisfying afternoon treats.

Basically, shortbread is some combination of butter and flour, worked together and flavored. Many excellent cooks believe that the best way to "work" the butter into the flour mixture is with your fingers, as it allows you to "feel" the dough, as it combines. A food processor, fitted with a metal disk, also does a good job of combining the butter with the flour mixture. If using this method, cut the butter into 1-inch (2.5-cm) cubes. Don't process the dough too much as it will destroy the "crumb".

Many cooks have shortbread tricks. When making sweet shortbread, some use extra-fine sugar (see Hint, page 182). Others swear by rice flour (see Hint, page 182). As you bake these shortbreads, you will soon get a feel for what techniques work best for you.

Ginger Shortbread

1 cup	softened butter	250 mL
1/2 cup	confectioner's (icing) sugar, sifted	125 mL
1/4 tsp	salt	1 mL
3 tbsp	finely chopped candied ginger	45 mL
2 cups	all-purpose flour	500 mL

Preheat oven to 300°F (150°C)
Ungreased 8-inch (20-cm) square pan

1. In a bowl, beat butter, sugar and salt until smooth and creamy. Mix in ginger until well incorporated. Gradually sift in flour, mixing well after each addition.

2. Press dough into pan and, using a fork, prick deeply all over. Bake in preheated oven for 50 to 60 minutes or until golden brown. Cool in pan for 5 minutes, then invert onto a cutting board. Using a knife, score 32 bars, 2x1 inch (5x2.5 cm). When cool enough to handle, using a lifter, transfer to wire racks to cool.

Makes 32 bars

Cheddar Shortbread

2 cups	all-purpose flour	500 mL
1 tsp	salt	5 mL
Pinch	cayenne (optional)	Pinch
1 cup	softened butter or margarine	250 mL
1 1/2 cups	shredded Cheddar cheese	375 mL

VARIATION

Food Processor Method
This method also works well and has the advantage of fully integrating the Cheddar into the dough. Cut butter into 1-inch (2.5-cm) cubes and place in freezer. In a food processor, using the metal blade, add flour, salt and cayenne. Pulse until blended. Add cheese and pulse until well combined. Add chilled butter and pulse just until a dough forms. Turn out on a floured board and knead lightly. Follow Step 3 right.

Preheat oven to 425°F (220°C)
Greased cookie sheet

1. In a bowl, combine flour, salt and cayenne, if using.

2. In another bowl, cream butter. Beat in cheese, using a spoon, until well blended. Gradually add flour mixture, mixing thoroughly after each addition. Turn out on a floured surface and knead lightly.

3. Shape dough into an 8-inch (20-cm) square and cut into 4x1-inch (10x2.5-cm) bars. Bake in preheated oven for 25 minutes or until golden brown. Immediately transfer to wire racks to cool.

Makes 32 bars

Refrigerator Nut Shortbread

3 cups	cake and pastry flour	750 mL
1/2 cup	rice flour	125 mL
3/4 cup	granulated sugar	175 mL
1 1/2 cups	softened butter	375 mL
	Finely chopped almonds or pecans	

HINT: Refrigerator dough cookies are very convenient because you can make the dough ahead of time. When you're ready to bake, you can slice and bake as many cookies as you like.

Preheat oven to 300°F (150°C)
Ungreased cookie sheet

1. In a bowl, combine flours and sugar.

2. In another bowl, beat butter until smooth. Gradually add flour mixture, mixing thoroughly after each addition. Knead lightly.

3. Divide dough in half and shape into two logs, each about 1 1/2 inches (4 cm) in diameter. Roll logs in nuts until evenly coated. Wrap tightly in plastic wrap and twist ends to seal. Chill in refrigerator for 1 to 2 hours until firm.

4. Cut dough into 1/4-inch (0.5-cm) rounds and place on cookie sheet. Bake in preheated oven for 20 to 25 minutes or until golden brown. Cool on cookie sheet for 5 minutes, then transfer to wire racks to cool completely.

Makes about 6 dozen

Cherry Nut Refrigerator Shortbread

1 cup	all-purpose flour	250 mL
1/2 cup	confectioner's (icing) sugar, sifted	125 mL
1/2 cup	cornstarch	125 mL
3/4 cup	chopped candied cherries	175 mL
1/2 cup	chopped pecans	125 mL
3/4 cup	softened butter	175 mL

Preheat oven to 375°F (190°C)
Ungreased cookie sheet

1. In a bowl, mix together flour, confectioner's sugar and cornstarch. Add cherries and pecans and mix thoroughly.

2. In another bowl, cream butter. Gradually add flour mixture, mixing thoroughly after each addition. Knead lightly. Shape dough into a roll about 1 1/2-inches (4-cm) wide. Wrap tightly in plastic wrap and refrigerate for at least 4 hours.

3. When ready to bake, cut roll into slices 1/4 inch (0.5 cm) thick and place on cookie sheet. Bake in preheated oven for 8 to 12 minutes or until golden brown. Immediately transfer to wire racks to cool.

Makes about 3 dozen

Orange Shortbread

1 cup	softened butter	250 mL
1/3 cup	berry sugar	75 mL
1/4 tsp	salt	1 mL
1 tbsp	grated lemon zest	15 mL
2 tbsp	grated orange zest	25 mL
2 cups	all-purpose flour	500 mL

NOTE: Berry or fruit sugar is extra-fine granulated sugar, which you can buy at most supermarkets. Many people believe it improves the quality of shortbread.

Preheat oven to 300°F (150°C)
Ungreased cookie sheet

1. In a bowl, beat butter and sugar, until smooth and creamy. Add salt and zests and blend in well.

2. Gradually add flour, mixing thoroughly after each addition. Knead lightly. Shape into a roll, wrap tightly in plastic wrap and refrigerate for at least 2 hours or overnight, if desired.

3. When ready to bake, cut dough into 1/4-inch (0.5-cm) slices and place on cookie sheet. Bake in preheated oven 10 minutes or until lightly browned. Immediately transfer to wire racks to cool.

Makes about 2 dozen

Chocolate Shortbread

3/4 cup	all-purpose flour	175 mL
1 tbsp	cornstarch	15 mL
Pinch	salt	Pinch
3 tbsp	unsweetened cocoa	45 mL
1/2 cup	softened butter	125 mL
1/2 cup	confectioner's (icing) sugar, sifted	125 mL
1/2 tsp	vanilla	2 mL

Preheat oven to 325°F (160°C)
Ungreased cookie sheet

1. In a bowl, sift together flour, cornstarch, salt and cocoa.

2. In another bowl, beat butter, confectioner's sugar and vanilla until smooth and creamy. Gradually add flour mixture, mixing thoroughly after each addition. Knead briefly.

3. Shape dough into 1-inch (2.5-cm) balls and place about 2 inches (5 cm) apart on cookie sheet. Using the bottom of a glass or the tines of a fork to make a criss-cross pattern, flatten slightly. Bake in preheated oven for 20 minutes or until firm. Cool slightly, then transfer to wire racks or waxed paper-lined platter to cool completely.

Makes about 2 1/2 to 3 dozen

Lemon Poppy Seed Shortbread

1 cup	all-purpose flour	250 mL
1/2 cup	confectioner's (icing) sugar, sifted	125 mL
1/2 cup	cornstarch	125 mL
2 tbsp	grated lemon zest	25 mL
1 tbsp	poppy seeds	15 mL
3/4 cup	softened butter	175 mL

HINT: Put lemon and orange zest in water, in a saucepan, and let simmer. You'll have a refreshing, wonderful aroma all through the house.

Preheat oven to 300°F (150°C)
Ungreased cookie sheet
Cookie cutters

1. In a bowl, mix together flour, sugar, cornstarch, lemon zest and poppy seeds.

2. In another bowl, cream butter. Gradually add flour mixture, mixing well after each addition. Knead lightly.

3. On a lightly floured surface, roll out dough to 1/4-inch (0.5-cm) thickness. Using cookie cutters, cut into desired shapes. Alternately, shape dough into 1-inch (2.5-cm) balls and flatten slightly with a fork and place on cookie sheets. Bake in preheated oven for 15 to 20 minutes or until lightly browned. Immediately transfer to wire racks to cool.

Makes about 2 dozen

Old-Time Oatmeal Shortbread

1 cup	all-purpose flour	250 mL
1/2 tsp	baking soda	2 mL
2 cups	quick-cooking rolled oats	500 mL
1 cup	softened butter	250 mL
1/2 cup	firmly packed brown sugar	125 mL
1 tsp	vanilla	5 mL

Preheat oven to 350°F (180°C)
Ungreased cookie sheet
Cookie cutters

1. In a bowl, mix together flour, baking soda and oats.

2. In another bowl, beat butter, brown sugar and vanilla until smooth and creamy. Gradually add flour mixture, mixing thoroughly after each addition. Knead lightly. Wrap tightly in plastic wrap and refrigerate for at least 2 hours.

3. On a lightly floured surface, roll out dough to 1/4-inch (0.5-cm) thickness. Using cookie cutters or a glass dipped in flour, cut into desired shapes and place on cookie sheet. Bake in preheated oven for 10 to 12 minutes or until golden brown. Immediately transfer to wire racks to cool.

Makes about 4 dozen

Original Scottish Shortbread

1 cup	softened butter	250 mL
3/4 cup	granulated or fruit sugar	175 mL
2 1/2 cups	sifted all-purpose flour	625 mL

VARIATIONS

Honey Shortbread Cookies
Reduce sugar to 1/2 cup (125 mL).
After beating butter and sugar,
add 1/4 cup (50 mL) liquid honey.

Butterscotch Shortbread Cookies
Use 1 cup (250 mL) firmly
packed brown sugar in place
of granulated sugar.

Preheat oven to 300°F (150°C)
Ungreased cookie sheet
Cookie cutter

1. In a bowl, beat butter and sugar until smooth. Gradually add flour, mixing thoroughly after each addition. Knead lightly. Wrap tightly in plastic wrap and refrigerate for 1 to 2 hours.

2. On a lightly floured surface, roll out dough to about 1/2-inch (1-cm) thickness. Using a cookie cutter or a glass dipped in flour, cut into desired shapes and place on cookie sheet. Bake in preheated oven for 20 to 25 minutes or until golden brown. Immediately transfer to wire racks to cool.

Makes about 3 dozen

Cream Cheese Shortbread

1	package (4 oz/125 g) softened cream cheese	1
1 cup	softened butter	250 mL
1/2 cup	granulated sugar	125 mL
1 tsp	vanilla	5 mL
2 cups	sifted all-purpose flour	500 mL

Preheat oven to 375°F (190°C)
Ungreased cookie sheet
Cookie cutters

1. In a bowl, beat cream cheese and butter until smooth. Add sugar and mix until creamy. Stir in vanilla. Gradually add flour, mixing well after each addition. Knead lightly.

2. On a lightly floured surface, roll out dough to 1/4-inch (0.5-cm) thickness. Using a cookie cutter or a glass dipped in flour, cut into desired shapes and place on cookie sheet. Bake in preheated oven for 8 to 10 minutes. Immediately transfer to wire racks to cool.

Makes about 3 dozen

Grandma's Traditional Shortbread

1/2 cup	confectioner's (icing) sugar	125 mL
1/2 cup	cornstarch	125 mL
1 cup	all-purpose flour	250 mL
3/4 cup	softened butter	175 mL

HINT: Give your shortbread a professional look by dipping the shapes into melted white or dark chocolate and then sprinkling the chocolate with finely chopped nuts.

Preheat oven to 300°F (150°C)
Ungreased cookie sheet
Cookie cutters

1. In a bowl, sift together sugar, cornstarch and flour.

2. In another bowl, cream butter. Using two knives, a pastry blender or your fingers, work flour in until a smooth dough forms. Knead lightly. Wrap dough in plastic wrap and refrigerate for about 30 minutes.

3. On a lightly floured surface, roll out dough to 1/4-inch (0.5-cm) thickness. Using cookie cutters or the top of a glass dipped in flour, cut into desired shapes and place on cookie sheet. Bake in preheated oven for 15 to 20 minutes or until lightly browned. Immediately transfer to wire racks to cool.

Makes about 2 dozen

Classic Xmas Shortbread

1 cup	softened butter	250 mL
2/3 cup	packed brown sugar	160 mL
2 cups	sifted all-purpose flour	500 mL

HINT: Dip the ends of plain short-bread cookies into melted chocolate. Let excess drip into saucepan, then place on a cookie sheet until chocolate hardens.

Preheat oven to 350°F (180°C)
Lightly greased cookie sheet
Cookie cutters

1. In a bowl, cream butter and brown sugar until smooth. Gradually add flour, mixing thoroughly after each addition. Knead lightly.

2. Shape dough into a ball. Roll out on floured working surface to about 1/4-inch (0.5-cm) thickness. Using cookie cutters or a glass dipped in flour, cut into desired shapes and place on prepared sheet. Bake in preheated oven for 12 to 15 minutes or until golden brown. Immediately transfer to wire racks to cool.

Makes about 3 dozen

Spicy Shortbread Wedges

1 cup	softened butter	250 mL
1 cup	packed brown sugar	250 mL
2 tbsp	grated orange zest	25 mL
1 tbsp	cinnamon	15 mL
3/4 tsp	cloves	4 mL
2 tbsp	ground ginger	25 mL
1 tsp	baking soda	5 mL
2 cups	all-purpose flour	500 mL
	Granulated sugar	

HINT: If a recipe calls for superfine sugar, whirl regular granulated sugar in a blender until fine.

Preheat oven to 325°F (160°C)
Two 8-inch (20-cm) round cake pans

1. In a bowl, beat butter, brown sugar, orange zest, cinnamon, cloves, ginger and baking soda until smooth and creamy. Gradually add flour, mixing thoroughly after each addition. Knead lightly.

2. Divide dough in half. Place half in one pan and press evenly over bottom. Repeat with remaining dough in second pan. Sprinkle tops with granulated sugar and bake in preheated oven for 25 to 30 minutes or until tops look dry and slightly crackled and edges are higher than the centers. Cool in pans for 5 minutes, then invert onto a cutting board. Cut each cake into 16 wedges.

Makes 32 wedges

Raisin Shortbread Wedges

1/3 cup	orange juice	75 mL
3/4 cup	seedless raisins	175 mL
1 1/2 cups	sifted all-purpose flour	375 mL
1/4 cup	granulated sugar	50 mL
1/2 cup	softened butter	125 mL

HINT: Some cooks believe the use of rice flour improves shortbread. Try substituting rice flour for one-fifth of the all-purpose flour in this or any other shortbread recipe.

Preheat oven to 350°F (160°C)
Greased cookie sheet

1. In a small saucepan, bring orange juice and raisins to a slow boil. Cover and cool, if possible, overnight.

2. In a bowl, mix together flour and sugar.

3. In another bowl, cream butter. Gradually add flour mixture, mixing thoroughly after each addition. Knead dough thoroughly.

4. Divide dough in quarters and shape into rounds, about 1/4 inch (0.5 cm) thick. Place one round on prepared cookie sheet and spread cooled raisin mixture over the entire surface. Top with another round, pressing down firmly. Using your fingers dipped in flour, pinch edges together. Prick entire top with a fork. Bake in preheated oven about 20 minutes or until golden. Mark into 8 segments as you would a pie, and when cool, remove from cookie sheet.

Makes 32 wedges

Shortbread Wedges
with Peanut Butter and Jam

1¼ cups	all-purpose flour	300 mL
½ tsp	baking powder	2 mL
¼ tsp	salt	1 mL
3 tbsp	softened butter	45 mL
½ cup	smooth peanut butter	125 mL
½ cup	granulated sugar	125 mL
1	egg	1
½ tsp	vanilla	2 mL
	Grape jam or jelly	

Preheat oven to 350°F (180°C)
9-inch (23-cm) round pie plate or quiche pan, sprayed with vegetable spray

1. In a bowl, mix together flour, baking powder and salt.

2. In another bowl, beat butter, peanut butter and sugar until smooth and creamy. Add egg and vanilla and beat until well blended. Gradually add flour mixture, mixing thoroughly after each addition. Knead lightly. Wrap dough tightly in plastic wrap and chill in refrigerator for several hours or overnight.

3. Press dough into bottom of prepared pan. Using a knife, score 18 pie-shaped wedges. (Do not cut all the way to the bottom.) Bake in preheated oven for 10 minutes. Using the tip of a wooden spoon press random grooves into the dough. Fill with grape jam or jelly and return to the oven for 8 more minutes. Place plate on a wire rack to cool. Cut into 18 wedges.

Makes 18 wedges

Whipped Shortbread

2 cups	softened butter, about 1 lb (500 g)	500 mL
1 tsp	vanilla	5 mL
½ cup	cornstarch	125 mL
3 cups	all-purpose flour	750 mL
1 cup	confectioner's (icing) sugar, sifted	250 mL
	Maraschino cherries (optional)	

Preheat oven to 300°F (150°C)
Ungreased cookie sheet

1. In a bowl, beat butter until smooth. Stir in vanilla. Add cornstarch, flour, confectioner's sugar and beat until dough is a smooth consistency resembling whipped cream.

2. Drop by teaspoonfuls (5 mL) about 2 inches (5 cm) apart onto cookie sheet. Bake in preheated oven for 15 minutes or until golden brown. Top with a maraschino cherry, if desired. Immediately transfer to wire racks to cool.

Makes about 9 dozen

Library and Archives Canada Cataloguing in Publication

Brody, Esther, author
  The 250 best cookie recipes / Esther Brody.

Includes index.
Originally published: Toronto : Robert Rose, 2001.
ISBN 978-0-7788-0468-0 (pbk.)

  1. Cookies. 2. Cookbooks. I. Title. II. Title: Two hundred fifty best cookie recipes.

TX772.B76 2013   641.86'54   C2013-902256-2

Index